DEVELOPING A HEALING MINISTRY

A TRAINING MANUAL FOR CHURCHES

John Coles

newwine

First Published in Great Britain in 2003 by New Wine
4A Ridley Avenue, Ealing, London, W13 9XW, England.
ISBN 1 902977 12 2

First Edition 2003
10 9 8 7 6 5 4 3 2 1 0

Acknowledgements
All scripture quotations are taken from the Holy Bible New International Version, copyright © 1973,1978,1984 by International Bible Society. Used with permission of Hodder and Stoughton a member of the Hodder Headline Group. All rights reserved. NIV is a trade mark of International Bible Society, UK trade mark number 1448790

A catalogue record for this book is available from the British Library

Type set & cover design, Mike Thorpe, Design Chapel
Printed in Great Britain by Gemini Print Services

Contents

Foreword

This booklet really needs no introduction. John Coles is well known as the leader who built up St. Barnabas, Woodside Park, North London, over twenty years and as my successor leading the now fast growing New Wine organisation.

We have all been greatly inspired and helped by the teaching and practice of the late John Wimber, the founder of the Vineyard Movement. Indeed New Wine was originally founded in 1989 to propagate many of Wimber's insights and practices. He had first brought his teaching and model for ministry to England in 1981. We immediately noted three significant elements from that visit.
1) Effective healing. 2) Involvement of the laity. 3) A new awareness of the role of the Holy Spirit in such ministry. And then we discovered a fourth significant factor – 4) This ministry could even operate and be developed in a traditional church – like the Church of England.

Over the years since then at New Wine, this ministry for healing and deliverance has been refined and now much of this wisdom has been incorporated in this booklet by John Coles. He writes very easily, lucidly and with the hindsight of long experience as he reaffirms the basics. It is important to have it all in print since sometimes sadly this kind of ministry has been abandoned because of serious mishandling. Sufferers who could greatly benefit from such a ministry when handled wisely, humbly and sensitively, have been put off by teaching and practices we could not endorse. And some leaders have also been alarmed, mistakenly fearing that involving the laity creates more problems than it solves. But since this ministry is part of the original mandate of the Lord to his Church, misuse is no excuse for disuse. The answer is right use!

This booklet is intended to provide some helpful guidelines and correctives to those who want to get it right and keep it right. Responsible lay folk will be only too ready to do all they can to correct mal-practices and to receive affirmation from such helpful biblical insights and experience.

May God bless each reader and give a double blessing to each practitioner!

I am delighted to commend this booklet

David Pytches July 2003

1 THE FOUNDATIONS OF THE HEALING MINISTRY

1.1 Rediscovering the Ministry of Jesus

Everyone knows that to be a Christian involves becoming more like Jesus. In our understanding this involves at least three things:

- Developing the type of relationship with God that Jesus had.
- Having our lives transformed by the Holy Spirit to lives of purity and holiness such as characterised Jesus' life.
- Ministering to people with the same love and power in which Jesus ministered.

Learning to minister like Jesus is as much a part of our discipleship as developing our relationship with God and as being transformed by the Spirit. They are like the three strands of a rope, designed to be intertwined to make our likeness to Jesus as strong as possible. Many of us have, for many years, focussed on only two of these strands. The result is that our likeness to Jesus is less than it could be, and our witness for Jesus is less effective than it could be. The desire to become 'more like Jesus' in every possible way underlies this booklet.

Healing is a broad field – it ranges from: physical to emotional; release from guilt and shame to deliverance; and healing past traumas to healing present hurts. There is much to learn. But Jesus promised that the Holy Spirit would lead his disciples into an ever deeper understanding and experience of the truth: *But when he, the Spirit of truth, comes, he will guide you into all truth. (John 16:13)*

It is our prayer that as you read this booklet the Holy Spirit will lead you further in the truth, and enable you to become 'more like Jesus'.

Proclamation and Demonstration

Jesus was committed to proclaiming the good news of God's Kingdom and love, and also to demonstrating the reality of that Kingdom through bringing healing to the sick, and freedom to the oppressed. The summary verses linking sections of Matthew's gospel together indicate the natural connection and balance between these things: *Jesus went through all the towns and villages, teaching in their synagogues, preaching the good news of the kingdom and healing every disease and sickness. (Matt 9:35)*

The 'motivation' behind his healings was his compassion. Healing was the natural expression of the outpouring of God's love into people's lives: *When Jesus landed and saw a large crowd, he had compassion on them and healed their sick. (Matt 14:14)*

As John Wimber used to say 'Jesus was a "word-worker" – his words proclaimed the reality of the Kingdom of God, and his works demonstrated the reality of it.'

Every Christian is called to learn to minister like this. Through the life of Jesus as told in the gospels there is a natural progression in the training and sending of more and more workers into the harvest-field.

First, Jesus himself did this work wherever went: *So he travelled throughout Galilee, preaching in their synagogues and driving out demons. (Mark 1:39)*

Then Jesus chose twelve others in order to train them. They were to be with him wherever he went, watching and learning how he preached and brought healing to the oppressed: *He appointed twelve – designating them apostles – that they might be with him and that he might send them out to preach and to have authority to drive out demons. (Mark 3:14-15)*

When the time was right Jesus sent out those he had been training – to minister to others in the same way that they had seen and heard him ministering: *When Jesus had called the Twelve together, he gave them power and authority to drive out all demons and to cure diseases, and he sent them out to preach the kingdom of God and to heal the sick. (Luke 9:1-2)*

Later Jesus commissioned a second wave of trainees to do the same thing: *After this the Lord appointed seventy-two others and sent them two by two ahead of him to every town and place where he was about to go. ... Heal the sick who are there and tell them, 'The kingdom of God is near you.' (Luke 10:1,9)*

Finally, Jesus entrusted to those he had trained in his lifetime the responsibility of teaching and training subsequent generations of believers to do exactly the same things: *Therefore go and make disciples of all nations, baptising them in the name of the Father and of the Son and of the Holy Spirit, and teaching them to obey everything I have commanded you. (Matt 28:19-20)*

It is clear that in the New Testament church this ministry was not just exercised by the apostles (the first twelve). They were the 'prototype' disciples, setting the pattern for all future disciples of Jesus. There are named and unnamed Christians, not part of the original twelve or seventy-two, who were given the same ministry: *So Paul and Barnabas spent considerable time there, speaking boldly for the Lord, who confirmed the message of his grace by enabling them to do miraculous signs and wonders. (Acts 14:3)*

This salvation, which was first announced by the Lord, was confirmed to us by those who heard him. God also testified to it by signs, wonders and various miracles, and gifts of the Holy Spirit distributed according to his will. (Heb 2:3-4)

It seems clear that it was Jesus' intention that the ministry of healing the sick should be a natural part of every Christian's life: *And these signs will accompany those who believe:...they will place their hands on sick people, and they will get well.(Mark 16:17-18)*

Francis MacNutt writes in his book *Power to Heal* (Hodder & Stoughton), 'It's only when thousands of ministers are praying for the sick that people will begin to regard the healing ministry as ordinary. Only then will the healer be regarded neither as an object of scorn, nor as a subject for worship.'

We are fortunate to live in an age when God is restoring this type of 'every member ministry', not just to church ministers, but to every Christian believer who is willing to learn about it. It is not a sort of optional extra for a few privileged, or highly spiritual, Christians. It is becoming an integral part of the life and ministry of many ordinary Christians. As a consequence the healing ministry is gaining visibility and credibility even in the Western world.

1.2 The Kingdom of God

Jesus' Central Theme

The central theme of all Jesus' teaching was 'The Kingdom of God'. By this he means 'The present rule and reign of a good God'. The good news that 'God is alive, powerful, and reigning' was the message that Isaiah said would characterise the ministry of the Messianic Servant of God, and his followers: *How beautiful on the mountains are the feet of those who bring good news, who proclaim peace, who bring good tidings, who proclaim salvation, who say to Zion, "Your God reigns!"* (Isa 52:7)

This kingdom is unlike all other kingdoms for it is not to be experienced only by those of a particular nationality, the Jews, or in a particular place, Israel, but by anyone who is willing to receive God's rule in their lives. This kingdom is a spiritual reality into which anyone can enter if they are born again by the Holy Spirit: *Jesus answered, "I tell you the truth, no-one can enter the kingdom of God unless he is born of water and the Spirit. Flesh gives birth to flesh, but the Spirit gives birth to spirit." (John 3:5-6)*

Jesus' first sermon introduces the key issues of the immediacy, the goodness and accessibility of the Kingdom to everyone: *"The time has come," he said. "The kingdom of God is near. Repent and believe the good news!" (Mark 1:15)*

In the type of teaching he used most often, namely the parables, Jesus would talk about the nature of the Kingdom, frequently speaking of its future growth: *He told them still another parable: "The kingdom of heaven is like yeast that a woman took and mixed into a large amount of flour until it worked all through the dough." (Matt 13:33)*

And in Jesus' personal prayer life, which became a model for our own, he prayed for the coming of God's Kingdom on earth: *This, then, is how you should pray: Our Father in heaven, hallowed be your name, your kingdom come, your will be done on earth as it is in heaven. (Matt 6:9-10)*

Jesus' last sermons were about the same themes, including the timing of the coming of the fullness of God's Kingdom: *He appeared to them over a period of forty days and spoke about the kingdom of God. (Acts 1:3)*

Moreover Jesus taught his disciples to spend their time and energy on being focused on the Kingdom of God rather than worrying about other things: *But seek first his kingdom and his righteousness, and all these things will be given to you as well. (Matt 6:33)*

The Kingdom of Darkness

The problem that most people have is that they neither experience the reality of the kind rule and reign of God in their lives, nor know of the goodness of God. Why not?

The Bible's answer is unequivocal: *The whole world is under the control of the evil one. (1 John 5:19): The devil, or Satan, 'leads the whole world astray'. (Rev 12:9)*

In one of his parables about the Kingdom, Jesus answers the question – 'how can there be so much evil in a world created by a good God?': *The owner's servants came to him and said, 'Sir, didn't you sow good seed in your field? Where then did the weeds come from?' ... 'An enemy did this,' he replied. (Matt 13:27-28)*

The truth is that there is a devil whose present activity, and ultimate aim, is to prevent people from recognising the love of God. Even in Jesus: *The god of this age has blinded the minds of unbelievers, so that they cannot see the light of the gospel of the glory of Christ, who is the image of God. (2 Cor 4:4)*

Satan exercises this scheming and destructive rule over everyone born into the world, and together with his malicious army of demons, is deeply opposed to everything Jesus Christ and his followers stand for: *Put on the full armour of God so that you can take your stand against the devil's schemes. For our struggle is not against flesh and blood, but against the rulers, against the authorities, against the powers of this dark world and against the spiritual forces of evil in the heavenly realms. (Eph 6:11-12)*

We do not want to over focus on the devil and his kingdom. Doing so can lead to either a preoccupation in him, or a fear of him, which is counterproductive. We can loose sight of God's power if we over focus on the power of the enemy. Yet we, like Paul, should not remain *'ignorant of his devices' (2 Cor 2.11 KJV)*.

A defining verse in understanding the mission of Jesus is found in one of John's epistles: *The reason the Son of God appeared was to destroy the devil's work. (1 John 3:8)*

The devil's work was to rebel against God, so usurping God's authority, and subsequently involving human beings in that rebellion, and all its consequences. The consequences of that fall, and the marks and signs of the devil's power in the world today are chiefly seen in:

Deception

This power is so great that people are deceived into believing they are free when in reality they are blind, unable to think clearly, or see the truth about God, or themselves: *The god of this age has blinded the minds of unbelievers, so that they cannot see the light of the gospel of the glory of Christ, who is the image of God. (2 Cor 4:4).*

Dominion of sin

Sin has a power over our lives from which it is humanly impossible to escape: *Scripture declares that the whole world is a prisoner of sin. (Gal 3:22)*

Sin has immediate and eternal consequences: *Whoever believes in him is not condemned, but whoever does not believe stands condemned already because he has not believed in the name of God's one and only Son. (John 3:18)*

Disease

The biblical view of the origin of sickness is that it is 'from the enemy'. This doesn't mean that every single sickness is the result of a demonic attack. It means that the environment we live in is so effected by the enemy that we no longer experience the presence of God in natural good health.

The difference between our future experience of heaven and our present environment on earth is that the enemy will not be present, nor have any effect, in the new creation. Heaven is a sickness-free zone because it is enemy free. Our present environment is, in one sense, enemy-controlled territory so we are all sickness-prone. This is clear from the Biblical picture of heaven: *He will wipe every tear from their eyes. There will be no more death or mourning or crying or pain, for the old order of things has passed away. (Rev 21:4)*

Demonisation

Sometimes the enemy's work results in serious physical symptoms, sometimes in emotional disturbance, and sometimes in behavioural or social problems. The enemy never plays fair. Although an ungodly life seems to invite his further assault, there are times when even the most godly people are assaulted to the point of despair by demonic attack – through no fault of their own: *So Satan went out from the presence of the LORD and afflicted Job... (Job 2:7)*

The enemy can also exercise his rule through demonic beings who are constantly seeking to assault, oppress, and invade people, and always with the intention of destroying their lives: *Your enemy the devil prowls around like a roaring lion looking for someone to devour. (1 Pet 5:8)*

Division

The increasing breakdown of society, the seemingly irreconcilable divisions in the nuclear family, between the generations, in local communities, in nations, and internationally, all originate from the enemy's destructive desires. It was never God's intention that we should experience such pain and loneliness in interpersonal or international relationships. The dividing wall separating people from each other has come from the enemy and can only be broken by the power of the Lord Jesus: *For he (Christ) himself is our peace, who ... has destroyed the barrier, the dividing wall of hostility,...*

His purpose was to create in himself one new man out of the two, thus making peace, (Eph 2:14-15)

Jesus was always welcoming into the new community of love that he was forming with his disciples, those that other religious people would normally have rejected.

Disaster

Throughout history 'natural disasters' have plagued, and will continue to plague human life: *When you hear of wars and rumours of wars, do not be alarmed. Such things must happen, but the end is still to come. Nation will rise against nation, and kingdom against kingdom. There will be earthquakes in various places, and famines. These are the beginning of birth-pains.* (Mark 13:7-8)

The Bible's view of such things is that they belong only to this fallen world. In the newly recreated heaven and earth there will be complete harmony between human beings and their environment: *The wolf will live with the lamb, the leopard will lie down with the goat, the calf and the lion and the yearling together; and a little child will lead them.* (Isa 11:6)

Death

Death too comes as a result of the fall, and is seen to be the last enemy of human beings. It has been overcome through the death and resurrection victory of Jesus, and will be given to all in Christ when he returns: *For since death came through a man, the resurrection of the dead comes also through a man. ...The last enemy to be destroyed is death.* (1 Cor 15:21, 26) The assurance of a future life beyond the grave can be received now through faith in Jesus: *Jesus said to her, "I am the resurrection and the life. He who believes in me will live, even though he dies; and whoever lives and believes in me will never die."* (John 11:25-26)

All these things, marks of the enemy's work, are things that Jesus came to overcome. This is what his ministry was all about, and what he spent his time doing. The gospels are full of the stories of how he overcame the destructive work of the enemy in each of these areas:

Kingdom of Darkness	Kingdom of God	
Deception	Truth and Light	John 3.21 – everyone; John 8.32-44 – religious people
Dominion of Sin	Forgiveness & Salvation	Mark 2.5 – the paralysed man; Luke 19.9 – Zacchaeus
Disease	Healing	Mark 10.52 – blind Bartimaeus; Matt 8.16 – everyone
Demonisation	Deliverance	Matt 12.22 – blind & mute man; Mark 5 – the man with Legions of demons
Division	Life & Community	Mark 2.14 – Levi, a tax-collector; Luke 7.37 – the prostitute
Disaster	Miracles	Mark 4.39 – stilling the storm; Matt 14.21 feeding the 5,000
Death	Resurrection	John 11.44 – Lazarus; Luke 7.15 – the widow's son

It was not just in his life and ministry that Jesus overcame the enemy in the lives of individuals. The decisive victory on behalf of everyone in Christ, was finally won through his death on the cross: *God forgave us all our sins, having cancelled the written code, with its regulations, that was against us and that stood opposed to us; he took it away, nailing it to the cross. And having disarmed the powers and authorities, he made a public spectacle of them, triumphing over them by the cross.* (Col 2:13-15)

On the cross Jesus inflicted a death-blow upon the enemy. Though strong, he is now bound, and his power is curbed (*Matt 12.29*). His doom is sealed, and the final victory of Jesus over all the power of the enemy is now in sight: *Then the end will come, when he (Christ) hands over the kingdom to God the Father after he has destroyed all dominion, authority and power. For he must reign until he has put all his enemies under his feet. The last enemy to be destroyed is death.* (1Cor15:24-26)

It is apparent that in one sense the Kingdom of God has already come. When Jesus cast out demons he could say: *But if I drive out demons by the Spirit of God, then the kingdom of God has come upon you.* (Matt 12:28)

Yet in another sense the Kingdom of God has not yet come. At the Last Supper Jesus spoke of the complete reign of God as something still in the future: *For I tell you I will not drink again of the fruit of the vine until the kingdom of God comes.* (Luke 22:18)

This fullness of the Kingdom of God comes when the Lord Jesus returns. That is why the Bible finishes with a prayer, expressing both our longing for Him, and our longing for an end to all the destructive activity of the enemy: *He who testifies to these things says, "Yes, I am coming soon." Amen. Come, Lord Jesus. (Rev 22:20)*

In a sense we live now in the 'in between times'. The power of the present ruler of this world has been broken – something of the power of the next world, of heaven itself, has broken in. We experience something of the future now. And every time we see someone saved, healed, or delivered we are seeing something more of that glorious future which one day everyone in Christ will experience. These things are signs of the kingdom and should impart faith that even more can happen as we pray: *Your kingdom come, your will be done on earth as it is in heaven. (Matt 6:9-10)*

If being a Christian involves becoming more like Jesus and learning to minister like him, then every Christian needs to learn how to bring the Kingdom of God into the lives of others. Doing so will involve us in overcoming the work of the enemy in the same areas as Jesus did. We do this through our proclamation of the simple gospel truth that 'our God reigns' (Isa 52.7), and at the same time, learning to pray for, expect, and minister in powerful signs and wonders : *For the kingdom of God is not a matter of talk but of power. (1 Cor 4:20)*

We will probably also discover that there are times when, despite our prayers, people are not healed or delivered, and disaster still strikes. On these occasions we find God's comfort both for ourselves, and those we are ministering to, in our understanding that the Kingdom is here now, and at the same time not yet fully here. This is a vital theological point for us to grasp if we are to persevere when the going is difficult. There are some things about God's plans and purposes which are still in the realm of mystery to us. Beyond our understanding now but about which we will have some understanding later: *Now we see but a poor reflection as in a mirror; then we shall see face to face. Now I know in part; then I shall know fully, even as I am fully known. (1 Cor 13:12)*

At all times, whether or not we are seeing great fruit in ministering healing, the primary marks of those who live in the Kingdom of God remain the same: *For the kingdom of God is not a matter of eating and drinking, but of righteousness, peace and joy in the Holy Spirit, (Rom 14:17)*

1.3 Power and Authority

For ordinary Christians to be involved in Healing Ministry they need to understand two foundational truths:

- God gives them authority for this ministry.
- The Holy Spirit empowers them for this ministry.

There are places in the Bible where the word 'authority' also implies 'power'. There are other places where the word 'power' also implies 'authority'. But there are passages where the two words, used together, must each mean something different. So people saw Jesus exercising both: *All the people were amazed and said to each other, "What is this teaching? With authority and power he gives orders to evil spirits and they come out!" (Luke 4:36)*

The word 'Authority' comes from the Greek 'Exousia'. It implies having the right to do something. For example a policeman in uniform bears the insignia of authority to apprehend members of the public behaving unlawfully. The word 'Power' comes from the Greek 'Dunamis'. It implies having the ability to do something. For example a warder with the keys has power to lock up or release a prisoner. To have authority without power is degrading. To have power without authority is dangerous. Jesus knew that he had both authority and power to bring healing to the sick. So must we.

Authority

Jesus' authority on earth – over everything in the created order – came from living under God's authority in his own life. This was an authority that God entrusted to the first human beings made in his image: *Then God said, "Let us make man in our image, in our likeness, and let them rule over the fish of the sea and the birds of the air, over the livestock, over all the earth, and over all the creatures that move along the ground." (Gen 1:26)*

In the Bible the fall is often seen as a rebellion against God's authority. The consequence is that we no longer know how to exercise that godly authority as God's vice-regents on earth. Only Jesus, who never rebelled against God's authority, naturally has that absolute Godly authority. So he had the God-given right to heal the sick.

This authority/right is what everyone who is born again by the Spirit is given. It is part of our birthright as Christians. In the prologue to John's gospel the word 'exousia' is used to describe the new status all Christians have in Christ: *Yet to all who received him, to those who believed in his name, he gave the right to become children of God. (John 1:12)* . This phrase could equally be translated, 'He gave to them the authority of children of God'. So, in Christ, the rightful place of human beings in and over the rest of creation is restored.

When Jesus sends the disciples ahead of him into the villages he makes this quite clear: *When Jesus had called the Twelve together, he gave them power and authority to drive out all demons and to cure diseases, (Luke 9:1)*

Jesus wants us to know that this is a ministry that all Christians have the authority to exercise. One of the means God uses to assure us of this God-given authority is through a process of commissioning and authorising in a public meeting. For some a single moment like this can release a lifetime's awareness of authority. For others there may need to be a series of such 'authorisations' before the penny drops. Sometimes we are bound by past negative teaching about the ministry of the Spirit and healing, and we need to be set free from this before we understand our authority to heal the sick.

At the same time as having this general authority, Jesus was also, moment by moment, dependent on instruction from his Father for when and how to engage in ministry. This was true both of what he said and when he said it: *For I did not speak of my own accord, but the Father who sent me commanded me what to say and how to say it. (John 12:49)*

And it was also true of when and how he ministered healing: *Jesus gave them this answer: "I tell you the truth, the Son can do nothing by himself; he can do only what he sees his Father doing, (John 5:19).* Jesus said this when he went to the Pool of Bethesda. There had been many sick people sitting around the pool. He only healed one paralysed man. It seems as if Jesus is saying that this was the one the Father had pointed out to him as being ready at that moment.

If we are to exercise our God-given authority in the same way that Jesus did, and to be used effectively in the healing ministry, then we need to cultivate lives similarly consecrated in obedience to God. We need to become as committed to holiness as Jesus was, and also as sensitive to the Father's daily prompting in ministry as Jesus was.

One of the reasons for our relative ineffectiveness in ministry, compared to Jesus, is our relative lack of obedience to the will of God in our lives.

This sensitivity to the prompting of the Father is also something we will need to cultivate if we are not to be exhausted by the constant and pressing needs which we will face. On one occasion we are told Jesus insisted in moving on, even when there were still people not healed: *At daybreak Jesus went out to a solitary place. The people were looking for him and when they came to where he was, they tried to keep him from leaving them. But he said, "I must preach the good news of the kingdom of God to the other towns also, because that is why I was sent." (Luke 4:42-43)*

Sometimes the expressed needs of people are what we must focus our time and energy on. But sometimes we need to learn to stop. This is where learning to obey God is more important than responding to people clamouring for our attention.

Power

Even though Jesus was wholly obedient from birth onwards, he did not exercise his ministry until after he was baptised in the power of the Spirit: *God anointed Jesus of Nazareth with the Holy Spirit and power, and .. he went around doing good and healing all who were under the power of the devil, because God was with him. (Acts 10:38)*

Sometimes Christians think that Jesus performed all the miraculous healing he did as a result of being divine (being incarnate as the second person of the Trinity). But at the start of this ministry Jesus himself gave the reason he was now engaging in this ministry:*"The Spirit of the Lord is on me, because he has anointed me to preach good news to the poor. He has sent me to proclaim freedom for the prisoners and recovery of sight for the blind, to release the oppressed, to proclaim the year of the Lord's favour." (Luke 4:18-19)*

This was recognised in the past by such as R A Torrey: 'Jesus Christ obtained power for his divine works not by His inherent divinity, but by his anointing through the Holy Spirit., He was subject to the same conditions of power as other men.' (*What the Bible Teaches*, p 94 Fleming H Revell Company)

If Jesus had healed the sick only because he was divine then there would be no possibility of the healing ministry being part of today's church (let alone the apostolic church). But if Jesus was a human being, empowered by the Spirit for this ministry, then there is the possibility that any of his followers might be similarly empowered for a similar ministry. This is exactly what Jesus was doing when he empowered the disciples to go into the villages ahead of him: *When Jesus had called the Twelve together, he gave them power and authority to drive out all demons and to cure diseases. (Luke 9:1)*

This empowering comes from the Holy Spirit: *But you will receive power when the Holy Spirit comes on you; (Acts 1.8)*

It is therefore vital that we do what we can to be filled, and refilled, with the empowering presence of the Holy Spirit. The filling of the Spirit is not something that is a one-off experience, either at conversion or on some other occasion. The disciples in the early Jerusalem church, who were filled with the Spirit at Pentecost (Acts 2:4), were filled again a few days later after they had prayed for Peter and John's release from prison (Acts 4:31). Paul was not only filled with the Spirit when Ananias prayed for him, (Acts 9:17) but also when he was ministering in Paphos (Acts 13:9). So the filling of the Spirit is something we need to pray for and seek on a continuing basis.

Another reason for our relative ineffectiveness in ministry, compared to Jesus, is that we are not filled with the Spirit 'without measure', as he was. It may help you to ask someone, who is obviously ministering in the power of the Spirit, to pray for you for a similar filling and impartation of the Spirit's power for ministering healing. Although we can, and should, pray for ourselves for this, it seems that God especially honours those who are humble enough to ask others to pray for them in this way.

Avoiding Abuse

Immediately following his baptism Jesus was led by the Spirit into the desert (*Luke 4:1-13*). Changing stones into bread might have satisfied immediate physical hunger, and leaping from the temple might have been a spectacular demonstration of power, but both would have involved abuse of this power. Jesus rejected the temptation to use his power outside the will of God.

The disciples were also tempted to abuse the power that had been given to them. Peter was offered money for his gift (Acts 8:18). James and John wanted to call down fire on Samaritan villages (Luke 9:54). Sadly, recent Christian history reveals that not all Christians empowered by the Spirit have resisted such a temptation. Some have misused the power or authority entrusted to them. Whenever Christians abuse these things the work of God is brought into disrepute in the eyes of both the church and the watching world.

As God entrusts an understanding of authority, and an experience of empowering we must be careful not to abuse his trust: *From everyone who has been given much, much will be demanded; and from the one who has been entrusted with much, much more will be asked.* (Luke 12:48)

1.4 Barriers to Involvement

If it is true that this healing ministry is something that every Christian is meant to exercise we must answer the question – 'Why aren't more people involved in this ministry today?'

There are many different factors which prevent people from being involved. Some will find themselves trapped by a number of them at the same time; others may be bound by only one. The power of each of them can be broken so that we are set free to minister as Jesus did.

Inadequate World View

A world-view is like a pair of glasses – everything we see in the world is seen through their lenses; they shape what we see, so that we 'interpret' the world in a particular way. It is normally such a natural part of us that we are unaware of it.

The world-view of the West in the second part of the 20th Century was based on scientific rationalism. Unless things could be explained logically or scientifically they could not be trusted as true. This meant there was great scepticism about the existence of God, the supernatural generally, and the possibility of miracles in particular. Through the 1990's this world-view was being replaced by post-modernity, which allows for a more personal appropriation of truth – in which truth is all relative to the experience of the 'traveller'.

For Bible-believing Christians any particular world-view needs to be weighed against the world-view revealed in the Bible. Doing this shows that a Christian world view is found neither in scientific rationalism nor post-modernity, though some elements of both may well be true. The Bible reveals a God who is both beyond reason and yet is reasonable. He is able to act in supernatural ways which are true to his character. In the context of healing we should note that one of the names by which God reveals himself in the Old Testament, and to which name he has bound himself to be faithful, is 'Jehovah Rophe': *I am the LORD, who heals you (Exod 15:26)*

The ways in which God brings healing are various:

• Through the natural healing properties God implanted in the human body as he created it. A cut finger will be healed 'all by itself' over a period of time if the cut is not infected.

• Through doctors. Medicine and prayer are not at odds with each other. The Bible has a very positive attitude to the medical practices of its day. Christians should have a similar attitude today. Their skills and wisdom in diagnosis and the discovery and prescribing of drugs are God-given, even though they are not always acknowledged to be so.

- Through the use of spiritual gifts (one of which is healings).
- Through prayer and faith.

Two of these means are open to reason and science; the other two are transrational. God is still the one who brings the healing – through whatever means he chooses to use. A Christian world-view must allow for the possibility of all of these means.

Sub-Biblical Theology

In the Western world there are two particular traps that many 'trained theologians' have frequently fallen into. The first is a liberal theological position based on scientific rationalism. Its starting point is that 'miracles cannot occur', and so it then reinterprets the miraculous stories of the Bible with other explanations. This is hardly taking Scripture seriously and is based on an erroneous world-view.

The second type of sub-biblical theology is cessationism. This is the view that the gifts of the Spirit, especially the supernatural gifts – such as tongues, healings, miracles etc – were God's gifts for the early church only. They then ceased to be part of normal church life once the Canon of Scripture was complete. This view is based on a belief that, those gifts and that ministry were needed at that stage of the church's life in order to authenticate the truth of what was being preached. According to this view, even after the canon of Scripture was complete, the stories of the miracles in the gospels were the only ones necessary to demonstrate Jesus is Saviour and Lord. 'We no longer need miracles to demonstrate to us the reality of the Kingdom of God'.

Though at one stage very popular in the Western world, this view has a number of key flaws.

First, it seems to be a theological justification for the experience of a miracle-less church, dominated by a faulty world-view. The answer to a faulty world-view is not to rewrite theology but to change the presuppositions on which the world-view is based. Start to believe in the possibility of the miraculous, and very quickly you will start to see the miraculous happening.

Second, there is no evidence in Scripture that the gifts would ever cease to be part of church life. In fact in 1 Corinthians 12 it seems to be implied that they will be here until the time of perfection comes; this is when Jesus returns, and not related to the Canon of Scripture being completed at all.

Third, in the light of the phenomenal growth in the Pentecostal and charismatic church worldwide during the 20th century, such a view is credible only if the experience of the miraculous of countless millions of Christians is discounted as self-delusion or demonic. If it is true that, *by their fruit you will recognise them (false prophets)'* (Matt 7.16), then the evidence of lives changed, people saved, healed and delivered, and the works of love and mercy bringing relief and help to the poor, seem to suggest the authenticity of these people's faith and these gifts as coming from our living God.

Fear

Fear is one of the 'key' seeds that the enemy sows into the lives of Christians in order to make them ineffective in serving the Lord. Fear of the healing ministry can grip us in a number of ways:

• 'What would happen if I prayed for someone to be healed and they weren't?' We have to be prepared to step out of the boat and obey the prompting of the Spirit. When we do that we leave the consequences to God. If we are obeying him then he is able to minister his love to people, even if they aren't immediately healed.

• 'What would happen if I tell someone "Our God heals" and he doesn't when I pray for them? Won't I damage their faith and God's reputation?' Provided we don't promise immediate healing when we talk about God as the healer, most people won't feel 'let down'. They will be blessed as we pray for them, and God is better at looking after his reputation than we are.

• 'What would happen if my people were to start praying for the sick – I wouldn't be able to cope with the pastoral difficulties this would raise if people aren't healed?' Such is the fear of many pastors that they won't, or don't, release their people into this ministry. The answer to abuse of any ministry is not non-use, but correct use. So there needs to be appropriate teaching and the authorising of a ministry team to ensure things are done 'decently and in order'.

These and other fears are based on lies of the enemy. They are best overcome by the teaching of Biblical truth, and by prayer ministry to release people from these misunderstandings.

Apathy

Sometimes non-believers seem to have more sympathy than Christians when people are sick. They will normally say something like, 'I hope that you get well soon'. This is a God-given reaction which still remains within people, despite the Fall. They say it out of concern and compassion.

What is present in non-believers ought to be present, in greater measure and understanding, in those who are now 'in Christ'. The life of the Spirit ought to be flowing out through us as it did through Jesus. So when we see someone who is sick our reaction ought to be that of Jesus: *When Jesus landed and saw a large crowd, he had compassion on them and healed their sick. (Matt 14:14)*

Perhaps some of us have lost the compassion that Jesus had. We have become apathetic to the pain and need of the broken lives of broken people who are all around us. Perhaps sometimes we even justify our apathy by talking about the priority of evangelism – so that we might 'save their souls'.

When the Spirit of God comes in power on people, they will normally find themselves having a renewed, God-given, compassion for others. This is evident in the manner in which they reach out to the poor in new ways, and pray for the sick to be healed. The apathy with which the enemy has entrapped them is replaced by the compassion of Jesus, with which the Spirit of God now empowers them.

Inappropriate Model

For many years there were three dominant models available to the church. These moulded the way most churches exercised the healing ministry. God has wonderfully used many of those who have pioneered or adopted one or another of these different approaches, and through them brought healing to many. But at the same time God is still wanting a vast army of his servants equipped to serve him in this way.

i) The sacramental model dominates the traditional churches. It is dependent on a properly trained and appointed leadership exercising this ministry in a highly controlled environment. Normally with a certain amount of accompanying religious practise and ritual. So healing might be administered at the Communion rail alongside communion, with the use of a liturgical prayer, and sometimes a liturgical response. While this has been effective for some, it limits the numbers of those ministering healing to those who have become suitably 'qualified'. It also limits the beneficiaries to those willing to go through the required spiritual hoops of church attendance and the like.

ii) The Eldership model is based on the instructions in the book of James (James 5.13-16). Any member of the church who is sick, and whose own prayers for recovery seem to be going unanswered, is invited to call for the elders of the church to come and pray for them. Sometimes anointing with oil accompanies the prayer. This model has the benefit of taking the healing ministry into the homes of believers, but sadly tends to keep the ministry in the hands of a small number of church members (only the elders), restricts healing to believers, and because it happens in homes rather than public church meetings, results in very little visibility for this ministry. The consequence is that in many churches it is rarely used except as a 'last resort'.

iii) The Pentecostal model dominates the Pentecostal and new churches. It is dependent on a highly anointed man or woman of God exercising this ministry, normally in a highly charged emotional environment, with a great emphasis on faith – almost 'faith in faith'. Again this ministry may be effective, but it seems to depend on 'superstars' It doesn't naturally and obviously result in releasing this ministry to ordinary Christians – in the way that Jesus envisaged. Moreover it seems to imply faith and emotion must go hand in hand, whereas in the New Testament faith is exhibited in different ways by different people. (See section 2.4).

John Wimber introduced many of us to a another model. This integrated model is the basis for the model for ministering healing in which New Wine has been training people over the last 15 years. It will be presented in section 2.1.

Conclusion

If you know that any of these, or other issues, have stopped you from committing yourself to a healing ministry, then you can be set free as you acknowledge the nature of the trap, repent (i.e. change your mind), and pray for release and freedom. It may help you to ask others to pray over you in a similar vein.

2 RELEASING THE MINISTRY

2.1 An Integrated Healing Model

There are two elements basic to this model. First, the example of Jesus himself. Second, the need to find a model that is appropriate in almost any context, and is possible for every Christian to follow. It is when the natural and supernatural combine, as they did in Jesus, that this ministry will gain its greatest credibility and reach most people.

At the heart of this model is a moment-by-moment dependence on the Holy Spirit. Healing ministry is about co-operating with God and what he is doing in a person's life as they come to him. It is vital that we regularly feed and nurture our relationship with God if we are to be able to be prompted by him while we are ministering and also to grow in our effectiveness in ministry.

General Tips

As you prepare to pray pay attention both to your spiritual relationship with the Lord, and to your behaviour and attitudes, your personal hygiene, and anything else which might adversely affect your physical relationship to the person being prayed for.

Wherever possible pray in pairs, including someone of the same sex as the sick person. Jesus sent the disciples out in pairs and we do well to follow this example – it helps both discernment and faith.

Ask the person what they want Jesus to do for them. We are helping them to reach out to receive healing from him. In doing this we are trying to get their attention away from us and onto the Lord – he is the only one who can heal anyone.

Explain how you will pray – this is especially important when praying for people who have had no previous experience of being ministered to for healing. Although you may be nervous they will be even more so – a little explanation can help allay their fears.

Pray with your eyes open, while encouraging the sick person to have their eyes closed. This will enable you to see whether the person is 'at ease' while being prayed for, and to see what God is doing while you are praying. (It can be hard to learn to pray with eyes open for those who are used to prayer meetings where bowed heads and shut eyes are the norm! But imagine Jesus on the road stopping to pray for the sick – when he touched their eyes or ears surely he would have had his eyes open.)

Lay hands carefully on the person in an appropriate way. Normally this should be gently on the shoulder or forehead and on the painful part of the person, provided that is appropriate. In some cases it is more appropriate to ask the person being prayed for to place their own hand on the painful part, if it is in a 'sensitive' area of their body.

Sometimes a person being prayed for may experience acute pain, or feel particularly hot or cold. These may indicate that God is 'doing something'. (All these things have their parallel in healing without prayer – manipulating a painful joint increases pain, using a sun-lamp causes great heat, and putting on an ice pack causes great cold!) If the hot or cold spot is under one of the hands of those praying move that hand to the painful part of the person being prayed for. (Again only do this if appropriate.) These signs are not conclusive evidence that God is healing. Sometimes a lot of heat is experienced and there is no apparent healing, and sometimes nothing is felt and yet healing may occur immediately, or follow later.

Never exert pressure on a person as if to push them over. Sometimes a person may fall under the power of this encounter with God, as happened to Abraham (Gen 17:3), Moses (Num 20:6), Daniel (10:9), John (Rev 1:17) and others. If this does happen, break their fall if possible and let them down gently. (Another good reason for keeping our eyes open is to see when this is happening so we can take the appropriate action – helping them to fall without harming themselves.)

A Model

What follows is not meant to be a rigid formula, but is intended as a guideline. It is based around five questions. We are principally asking these questions of God, although we can also address some of them to the person we are ministering to. We are expecting revelation from God, as well as information from the sick person.

The Interview – What's the problem?

Ask the sick person what ministry is wanted. Jesus sometimes asked this even when the answer seemed obvious. When he ministered to the blind men he asked: *"What do you want me to do for you?"* (Matt 20:32)

Follow up with further questions, such as 'How long have you had this problem?' – 'Has it been diagnosed by a doctor?' – 'Are you taking medication?' A long medical explanation from the sick person is not necessary – we are not doctors! But as the person begins to answer be asking the Lord 'what is the root of the problem?'

The Diagnosis – Where does it come from?

People are sick for a variety of reasons. The root of the sickness could be:

A purely physical sickness

Association with some trauma

Psychosomatically induced

A result of sin (eg sexually transmitted diseases)

A generational sickness within the family

A consequence of a demonic oppression

The result of a curse

The person may give us some clue as to the root cause of the problem if we sensitively ask some further questions, as the Spirit prompts: 'Were the symptoms preceded by any emotional shock or trauma (E.g. A death, a divorce, a separation, or loss of a job etc.)?'

At the same time we should be praying silently for discernment in case the real problem is unrepented sin or suppressed shock or grief, etc. We may not get any direct clue immediately from either the Lord, or the sick person, but we can still continue. The answer to this question may become clear as we progress. We must be careful not to insist we are right in our perception, and if we sense it is the result of some sin we must never be accusative or condemning. It is better simply to encourage some 'heart searching' and seeking of forgiveness 'for anything the Lord reveals to you'.

Prayer Selection – How shall I pray?

Our normal starting point is to invite the Holy Spirit to come with his power to heal. Then we wait, while praying silently in tongues, if that gift has been released in you. (The use of tongues in healing is significant. First, it helps to tune in to the Lord, and what he is saying or doing. Second, as we pray in tongues the Spirit himself is praying through us in a focussed and relevant way, even when we don't know precisely how to pray.) It is better to intercede silently in tongues. Praying aloud in tongues can be very off-putting to the sick person. We want them to concentrate on Jesus – not our prayers. We must not be surprised if, at this point, the enemy comes to put us out of action with temptations which make us feel ashamed, or feelings of uselessness which make us feel unworthy and not up to the task.

From now on it is important to 'track' the Holy Spirit during the time of prayer ministry, and to pray in other ways as he prompts.

Many of us learn to pray intercessory prayers at an early stage of our Christian life. But when Jesus ministered healing his prayers were quite different. He often addressed the illness or the person directly as the power of God flowed through him.

So we need to learn how and when to pray as Jesus did.

Touch and command: *Jesus reached out his hand and touched the man. "I am willing," he said. "Be clean!" And immediately the leprosy left him. (Luke 5:13)*

Declaration: *Hearing this, Jesus said to Jairus, "Don't be afraid; just believe, and she will be healed." (Luke 8:50)*

Rebuke: *So he bent over her and rebuked the fever, and it left her. She got up at once and began to wait on them. (Luke 4:39)*

Command: *For Jesus had commanded the evil spirit to come out of the man. (Luke 8:29)* It is probably best to say these words overtly in the name of Jesus, ie 'I command this fever in the name of Jesus to be gone.'

During this time keep:

Acknowledging, blessing, honouring and thanking God for all that he is doing.

Asking God to keep increasing his power to heal.

Being open to the manifestations of the Spirit's power – shaking, weeping, falling etc. If the sick person is unfamiliar with these things it is good to interpret them. E.g. 'That is the power of God – he is at work here'.

Quietly asking the Lord for more revelation to know how to pray more precisely.

Taking Stock – What's happening?

There could be four possible effects of our prayers (cf MacNutt):

i) Immediate healing – in which case give thanks and glory to God.

ii) Partial healing – as with the blind man: *He took the blind man by the hand and led him outside the village. When he had spat on the man's eyes and put his hands on him, Jesus asked, "Do you see anything?" He looked up and said, "I see people; they look like trees walking around." Once more Jesus put his hands on the man's eyes. Then his eyes were opened, his sight was restored, and he saw everything clearly. (Mark 8:23-5)*

We discover this by asking at some stage 'What is happening? – is there any improvement?', while at the same time encouraging them to keep their eyes closed. If there has been pain when a part of the body is moved, or loss of mobility, encourage them gently to try the same movement again to see if there has been any change in the symptoms. More ministry might be necessary either on this occasion or at another time. Always give the sick person the option of continuing or stopping the ministry at any stage, and always give them some idea of when they can be prayed for again.

iii) Delayed healing – as with the leprous men. They were healed as they left Jesus, rather than while they were with him: *When he saw them, he said, "Go, show ourselves to the priests." And as they went, they were cleansed. (Luke 17:14)*

Sometimes healing is progressive over a period of time – we may pray for them regularly and frequently, and the healing may come gradually over a period of a few weeks. (Francis McNutt encourages this approach to what he calls 'soaking prayer'.)

iv) No healing. Sometimes it appears as if nothing has happened. Be careful not to say that a person is healed when plainly they are not. Normally, even if there is no change in the presenting condition, the Lord has been ministering to the person in some other area of their life. Try to discern what this has been so that the person can leave encouraged by God's love and grace. At the same time, if the presenting condition is unchanged, offer another opportunity for prayer on another occasion

Post-prayer Advice – Where do we go from here?

It is important to know when and how to conclude a time of prayer ministry. We need to be sensitive to the person and their desires, and at the same time to the Lord, and what he is doing.

Even if it appears a person is healed we don't tell them to come off any medication a doctor has prescribed. If they are really healed their body will begin to react against the medication and it is the doctor's job to lower the dose or stop the treatment completely.

Sometimes a person appears to be healed when we pray for them, and then the symptoms reappear later. What then? More prayer is needed! We should first encourage a person in how to pray effectively for themselves by:

Remembering what God did previously and thanking him for the reality of that healing.

Resisting the return of the symptoms – refusing to accept back what God has taken away.

Then if the symptoms continue to reappear encourage them to ask others to pray with them once again for the healing to return and remain.

If a person doesn't exhibit any measure of healing it is vital to help them to know that God is still for them and not against them. They might easily feel guilt for not being healed – if there has been an over emphasis on faith they can feel guilty that it is their lack of faith that has kept them unhealed. If this happens their state is now worse since they are sick spiritually as well as physically!

Try to leave everyone with an assurance of God's loving presence, and the knowledge that he will never abandon them.

Help them to know that they can go on praying for their healing on their own. This is better, and more biblical advice, than telling them to 'go and claim your healing'. Healing is a gift from God as a result of his grace and mercy. We need to beware of not misreading the priorities on God's agenda for each person for whom we pray.

Offer them the opportunity for more prayer ministry. 'We would love to pray for you again', is an invitation that helps people to know there is no shame in not yet being healed. (This is not an offer of a private appointment, but of another opportunity in the church's calendar, and building.)

Sometimes it is useful to give people some words of Scripture to hold onto, and with which to build their trust in God's goodness. Alternatively, God may have given words of knowledge or prophecy during the prayer ministry which can be held on to, and prayerfully applied over the following days.

Conclusion

After prayer, whenever possible, encourage full involvement in the healing community of the local church. Healing can come through times of public worship, fellowship, restoration of relationships, and good teaching, as well as through further prayer ministry. Participation in the regular life of the local church is the best way of continuing to grow into the wholeness that Jesus wants his disciples to know, and be known for.

2.2 Sensitivity To The Holy Spirit

The Gifts of the Spirit

This healing ministry is the work of God. We cannot heal anyone in our own strength. So we need to develop our sensitivity to the Spirit, and his gifts, as we minister. Jesus used many of the gifts of the Spirit when he healed people. For instance, in the healing of the paralysed man (Mark 2), we see the gifts of discernment, knowledge, wisdom, faith, and miracle coming in quick succession as the Spirit of God prompted and equipped him in this healing encounter.

In 1 Corinthians 12 Paul outlines a number of the supernatural gifts, or gracings of the Spirit, with which God wants to equip the church. Churches today need to train their people in the right understanding and use of these gifts of the Spirit. Every Christian has the Holy Spirit living within them, and thus has the potential to exercise all the gifts of the Spirit. Paul speaks of the availability of all these gifts to the church, as members of the church ask for the release of the gifts. As the church meets together God gives these manifestations of the Holy Spirit through those he wishes to use on that particular occasion: *God gives them to each, just as he determines. (1 Cor 12:11)*

Over a period of time different members of the church begin to develop skills in the use of some of these gifts – such that they can be thought of as having a particular ministry in the church. God is thereby appointing people to longer term roles: *God has appointed ... workers of miracles, also those having gifts of healing ...(1 Cor 12:28)*

It is important to grasp this distinction between the manifestations – the gifts of the Spirit available to any Christian at any time as the Spirit wills – and the ministries that emerge over time under the empowering of the Spirit. Often Christians don't realise that they can learn how to use all the gifts as the need for them arises in particular ministry situations. At the same time, each of us also needs to know what our long term ministry role within the body of Christ is (Eph 4:11-13).

How does revelation work? In addition to the biblical precedents of dreams, visions, trances, voices, angelic visitations and heavenly raptures, it appears that God's people can discern God's revelation through the 'spiritual' senses.

Revelation

We can receive 'revelation' or 'knowledge' from God through:

feeling things; hearing things (Samuel and Saul of Tarsus); seeing things (words, names &; pictures, etc); knowing things; speaking things; smelling or tasting things.

These promptings of the Spirit can be 'like the flutter of a butterfly's wings'. They come so quickly, and are gone almost before we realise they are there. It is very easy to rationalise them away as being 'made up'. It requires a degree of faith in taking the risk of verbalising what you think the Spirit has said; but if you don't 'try it' sometimes you will never know whether it really was the Lord.

Whenever we sense God revealing something to us through any of these means we must remember, as with any of the gifts of the Spirit, we could be wrong; revelations need sifting, weighing, etc. So we should offer any words we receive with great sensitivity. We can have confidence in asking God for wisdom in knowing how to do this: *If any of you lacks wisdom, he should ask God, who gives generously to all without finding fault, and it will be given to him. (James 1:5)*

Christians have often been released into one of more of these gifts and then got stuck there. In our experience the ability to use each gift comes most often at a time of need, when a person expresses a desire for that particular gift, and through making themselves available to be used in that particular way by God. So each gift can be specifically prayed for, in faith received, and then in trust humbly exercised. Just as many are released in tongues through the laying on hands and with prayer so too can the other gifts be similarly imparted. It is apparent that gifts were imparted to Timothy in this way (2 Tim 1:6).

Those involved in ministering healing should be regularly asking God to release in them the necessary gifts in ever increasing measure.

The Work of the Holy Spirit

The gifts of the Spirit are not the only aspects of the Spirit's work that are important in this ministry. Amongst other aspects of the Spirit's ministry to remember as a church commits itself to releasing this healing ministry are:

• The Holy Spirit is our teacher in all things: *But when he, the Spirit of truth, comes, he will guide you into all truth. (John 16:13)* Consequently we can be sure that He will guide us in all the decisions we have to make over the right exercise of this ministry

• The Holy Spirit glorifies Christ: *He will bring glory to me by taking from what is mine and making it known to you. (John 16:14)* When the healing ministry is properly exercised more people will recognise Jesus as the Lord, be more grateful to him for all that he has done for them, and be more passionate about serving him.

• The Holy Spirit will come if we ask: *If you then, though you are evil, know how to give good gifts to your children, how much more will your Father in heaven give the Holy Spirit to those who ask him!" (Luke 11:13)* If we ask then the Father will give us the Spirit and his gifts to enable us to exercise this ministry.

• The Holy Spirit acts dynamically in the local church: *Now to each one the manifestation of the Spirit is given for the common good.... All these are the work of one and the same Spirit, and he gives them to each one, just as he determines. (1 Cor 12:7,11)* He is longing to be as generous to, and through, members of the church today as He was then. The ministry of the gifts of the Spirit is for everyone's benefit – so it is not to be feared but welcomed.

• The Holy Spirit has a part for everyone to play: *The body is a unit, though it is made up of many parts; and though all its parts are many, they form one body.* (1 Cor 12:12) Often when this ministry is introduced some in the church will be tempted to feel superior, because they are being 'used by God'. Others can be made to feel inferior, because they have a less supernatural ministry. The Holy Spirit doesn't give everyone public and visible roles. It is important for the church leaders to recognise this and to honour those who are engaging in less visible ministries – such as 'the gift of helping others', or mercy ministry. These are equally important in helping to make the Kingdom of God good news. *Each one should use whatever gift he has received to serve others, faithfully administering God's grace in its various forms. (1 Pet 4:10)*

• The Holy Spirit still speaks to the Churches today: *He who has an ear, let him hear what the Spirit says to the churches. (Rev 2:7)* If we were to go wrong, or get our priorities wrong, then the Lord is perfectly able to correct us today, just as he did the early church.

The Fruit of the Spirit

It is vital that those committed to being involved in this healing ministry understand the need to keep bearing the fruit of the Spirit in their lives: *The fruit of the Spirit is love, joy, peace, patience, kindness, goodness, faithfulness, gentleness and self-control (Gal 5:22)*

When the power and gifts of the Holy Spirit come upon a church, or an individual, it is easy to be mesmerised by the wonder and newness of these things. Sometimes there is a consequent loss of focus on the need to be continuously changed into living lives of purity like Jesus did.

The Corinthian church was gloriously open to the gifts of the Holy Spirit, but seemingly wasn't always using them wisely. Paul had to write in firm terms to remind them of the importance of only exercising these gifts in the context of love: *If I speak in the tongues of men and of angels, but have not love, I am only a resounding gong or a clanging cymbal. If I have the gift of prophecy and can fathom all mysteries and all knowledge and if I have a faith that can move mountains but have not love, I am nothing. (1 Cor 13:1-2)*

2.3 Foundational Values

In the early church using the gifts of the Spirit when the church gathered for worship had to be subject to order: *But everything should be done in a fitting and orderly way. (1 Cor 14:40)* Also in the church today there must be some clear order and understanding as to how those authorised to minister are to exercise this ministry, under the authority of the church's leadership.

Having too many rules runs the danger of killing the ministry, *'the letter kill' (2 Cor 3:6).* It is better to have common values which are accepted by all those involved in this ministry. These are some of the values we have found most important to emphasise within the church, and within the lives of those authorised to minister healing.

Each of these is something that the church should value together, and to which individuals should be personally committed if they are to be part of a church's authorised team. If a church leader authorises people onto the team who do not hold the church's values they are setting up the possibility of conflict which will grieve the Spirit and damage the ministry of healing.

The Person and Work of Christ

A church first needs to honour the uniqueness of Jesus and his sacrificial work upon the cross, atoning for human sin and overcoming the works of the enemy.

Jesus is the one who shows us in a unique way what God is really like – no-one else has done, or could do this: *No one has ever seen God, but God the One and Only, who is at the Father's side, has made him known. (John 1:18)*

When we see Jesus so committed to healing the sick we know that God's heart, mind, will and strength is committed to healing. To deny this is to deny and dishonour the unique revelation of God that Jesus has given us. Anyone who studies the gospels, and sees Jesus healing the sick, is seeing the eternal heartbeat of God: *Jesus answered: ...Anyone who has seen me has seen the Father. (John 14:9)*

The character of God is no different today than it was in Jesus' day. He is unchanging in his nature. He is equally committed to healing the sick today as he was then. Knowing this gives those ministering healing in his name confidence that he will – as they pray in faith in the name of Jesus.

Moreover we are told that on the cross Jesus has overcome all the powers of darkness, which includes the power of sickness, suffering, and death. It is for this reason that the prophet Isaiah was able to say: *But he was pierced for our transgressions, he was crushed for our iniquities; the punishment that brought us peace was upon him, and by his wounds we are healed. (Isa 53:5)*

Some, when speaking about and ministering healing, place their main emphasis on the fact that it is readily available to us here and now in the cross. Their conclusion is that it can be 'claimed', and then experienced, with an equal certainty of God giving it as with the forgiveness of sins and eternal salvation. This does not seem to be implied by the text, and there is no evidence in the New Testament that the early Christians believed this. It is better to say that the cross opens up all the blessings of heaven to us (Eph 1:3); we enter the Kingdom of God only as a result of it. We can immediately be assured of our eternal salvation, and our eternal healing, but we may have to wait for some time, even to the resurrection itself, before we experience the full wonder of either.

When ministering healing it is always good to thank Jesus for his power to heal, and for his death on the cross through which healing comes. This both honours the Lord and builds our faith as we minister.

No-one should be considered for this ministry who does not have a personal relationship with the Lord – having already experienced his forgiveness and regeneration. Additionally, the more a person is conscious of what Jesus has done for them on the cross, the more able they will be to minister the power of the cross to others.

More could be said about this, but we are assuming that most readers will already be clearer on the central place of Jesus in their lives, than on the significance of the other values we address now.

The Word of God

All Scripture is God-breathed and is useful for teaching, rebuking, correcting and training in righteousness, so that the man of God may be thoroughly equipped for every good work (2 Tim 3:16-17).

The Bible is our guide book in every aspect of Christian life and ministry. It is through our study of the Bible, and as God reveals himself to us through it, that we find our theology and model for healing ministry. All that is written in this booklet must be tested against the Scriptures to demonstrate its truthfulness.

The Bible speaks to us of our authority for healing as we minister in the name of Jesus. We are not claiming any authority for ourselves in this generation which Bible-reading and believing Christians have not deduced previously. We are not discovering a healing ministry, but rediscovering that which the Bible tells us Jesus entrusted to his first prototype disciples.

The Bible reminds us of the context for healing – the Preaching of the Cross and the Kingdom of God. For Jesus, healing always accompanied his proclamation of the good news of God's Kingship, love and power. In the early church, as the good news was taken from place to place, signs and wonders went alongside the proclamation of the gospel. Healing ministry must never replace the proclamation of the gospel – they go hand in hand.

The Bible gives us good models – that of Jesus in the gospels and the early Christians in the book of Acts. If we follow these models we will avoid the bizarre practises that can characterise some healing ministries.

The Bible also warns against abuses, such as greed: *Simon said, "Give me also this ability so that everyone on whom I lay my hands may receive the Holy Spirit." (Acts 8:19)*

Those involved in this ministry should be committed to meditating on the Scriptures, asking God to speak through them, and to letting the Scriptures fashion all their attitudes and every aspect of their lifestyles, as well as forming their understanding and practise of the healing ministry.

Wholeness

May God himself, the God of peace, sanctify you through and through. May your whole spirit, soul and body be kept blameless at the coming of our Lord Jesus Christ. (1 Thess 5:23)

This word 'whole' is derived from the Greek word 'sozo'. Used frequently in the gospels, it is sometimes thought to refer simply to the idea of eternal salvation, which God offers every individual through Christ (Mt 1:21). But it is much broader – it includes such concepts as:

• Holiness: *Make every effort to live in peace with all men and to be holy; without holiness no one will see the Lord. (Heb 12:14)*

Our sanctification is an integral part of our wholeness. In the Bible the command to be holy is frequently repeated *"Be holy because I am holy" (1 Peter 1:16)*. If a church is to be a place where the Holy Spirit is free to minister, there must be a real commitment to purity and holiness.

• Unity: *Make every effort to keep the unity of the Spirit through the bond of peace. (Eph 4:3)*

Harmonious loving relationships are meant to be the hallmark of the church: *By this all men will know that you are my disciples, if you love one another. (John 13:35)* When relationship are fragmented through unforgiveness, jealousy, competition and the like, the 'shalom' of the Christian community is destroyed and healing is inhibited.

• Maturity: *Until we all reach unity in the faith and in the knowledge of the Son of God and become mature, attaining to the whole measure of the fullness of Christ. (Eph 4:13)*

This means we all need to take responsibility for our own acts – owning our own bad decisions and no longer blaming others. Although we should always be childlike in our attitude, we should never be childish in our emotions and relationships.

• Healing: Sometimes the Greek word sozo is also used when Jesus healed sick people, or set the demonised free. So wholeness involves our coming to Jesus for healing also.

• Suffering: Our theology for both healing and suffering comes from our understanding that the Kingdom of God is already present in part, but not yet fully here. And our primary example for living in this in-between times is Jesus, who *'learned obedience from what he suffered'* (Heb 5.8). If we are to go on believing in the goodness of God we need to have a good understanding of the present partial nature of the Kingdom of God,and of the place of suffering in our lives, and that of others. This is the only way to avoid the despair that would otherwise overwhelm us as we live in a world in which there is so much untold suffering and injustice.

Consequently those involved in ministering healing should be committed to: growing in purity, maintaining loving relationships, maturing in every area of their lives, receiving prayer for their own healing, and to be learning how to respond in a Christlike manner to suffering and difficulty in their life. *No discipline seems pleasant at the time but painful – but later on it produces a harvest of righteousness and peace for those who have been trained by it.* (Heb 12: 11)

Love for the Individual

Every individual is of infinite value to God, and we need to learn to view each person in the same way that God views them.

• God knows us all personally by name: *He calls his own sheep by name and leads them out. (John 10:3)*

• God knows the number of hairs on our heads: *And even the very hairs of your head are all numbered. (Mat 10:30)*

• God measures our tears: *Record my lament; list my tears on your scroll – are they not in your record? (Psa 56:8)*

On one notable occasion Jesus was prepared to stop everything because he noticed that someone in the crowd had touched his robe and that healing power had left him. (Luke 8:43-48) He was not prepared to go on without finding out who it was and commending her. Such is his care for the individual.

In our prayer ministry we need to develop and express a similar sensitivity for each individual. A good rule of thumb in ministry is not to do anything to someone else that we wouldn't like done to us! This would probably avoid much of the bad practice of loud shouting while ministering!

In particular we need to learn to treat individuals with:

Empathy and compassionate love. *"Love your neighbour as your self"* (Luke 10:25-37)

A willingness to listen and take them seriously. *Everyone should be quick to listen, slow to speak (James 1:19)*

Acceptance and without harsh judgment: *Accept one another, then, just as Christ accepted you (Rom 15:7)*

Respect and dignity. *Honour one another above yourselves. (Rom 12:10)*

Humility and gentleness. *Be completely humble and gentle; be patient, bearing with one another in love. (Eph 4:2)*

Sometimes people can become almost dependent on the prayer ministry of others. We need to recognise this possibility and keep reminding people to take responsibility for their own personal growth. The Lord wants each of us to seek him and receive from him personally, not just through the prayers and words of others.

Consequently those involved in ministering healing should be people who are willing to learn to be sensitive to people.

The Body of Christ

The local church fellowship is the best place to learn how to minister healing. It is here that we are called to enter into loving and accountable relationships, both with our peers, and those in leadership.

It is also in our local church that we should have friends who are committed both to this healing ministry, and to seeing us grow in maturity in Christ. These are the sort of friends who can correct us if we misuse the gifts. None of us particularly like being corrected – it is painful, but through it we grow: *Wounds from a friend can be trusted, (Prov 27:6)*

In the church there is also an appointed leadership who are accountable to God for the right ordering of the church's life and ministry. They want to ensure this healing ministry is exercised in a right way. Proper respect for the leadership of the church is to the advantage of everyone: *Obey your leaders and submit to their authority. They keep watch over you as men who must give an account. Obey them so that their work will be a joy, not a burden, for that would be of no advantage to you. (Heb 13:17)*

In order to ensure that the guidelines and values to which the church ascribes are being adhered to, a wise church leader will regularly review the practices of the team with the team leader. From time to time it may be necessary to speak to individuals on the team if they are departing from these practices and introducing other values. If this is not done, then over a period of time the ministry will dry up because people will no longer know in what way they will be ministered to if they come for prayer. Some sort of quality control needs to be exercised over the ministry offered.

Sometimes, although someone may be highly gifted in prayer ministry, they may be running away from other issues in their lives, or falling into temptation and sin. In these cases it may be necessary to ask someone to stop being part of the team for a while until those other issues are dealt with. It is tempting to avoid the sort of conflict that this type of action can bring, but in our experience failure to do this brings the healing ministry into disrepute.

Consequently, those involved in ministering healing should be people who are willing to follow the guidelines and values set by the church leadership, and open to the gentle correction of the church's leaders. The church leader should host occasional ministry team meetings for feedback, revue, teaching, fresh empowering and reiteration of values.

There is one other thing about ministering healing in the local church. 'The meeting place is the learning place for the market place' (David Pytches). It is not God's intention that we should only minister healing in church meetings. God wants us to be ministering healing in our homes, in hospitals, and wherever we meet sick people. What we do, and the way we do it, when as Christians we gather in the meeting place, will determine both what we do and the way we do it with those we meet in our daily lives (the market place). For that reason we need to learn how to do this ministry effectively, and in a non-religious way, so that we can confidently offer prayer to anyone, believer of not, anywhere, at any time. (If in contrast we allow strange prayer practises to develop in church we will never take this ministry onto the streets. This is where Jesus did it in his day, and where he wants us to take it today.)

Prayer

God has bound himself to certain principles regarding the way he works in his world. Although he is Almighty he has chosen to work through weak and mortal human beings. It seems as if the weaker, and more childlike we are, the more he is glorified: *But we have this treasure in jars of clay to show that this all-surpassing power is from God and not from us.* (2 Cor 4:7)

God has promised that he will answer the prayers of his people – he has bound himself to hear and respond to those who wholeheartedly seek him: *You will seek me and find me when you seek me with all your heart.* (Jer 29:13)

This is true for individuals who call upon him for themselves, and also for churches who call upon him together, asking that their church might become a vibrant life-giving and healing community, such as the first church was.

There are four important applications in the realm of prayer for healing.

It is true for individuals who come forward for prayer as they earnestly seek God. We need to encourage people to pray for their own healing, not just to come and be prayed for by others. The kingdom of God advances as people seize it: *From the days of John the Baptist until now, the kingdom of heaven has been forcefully advancing, and forceful men lay hold of it.* (Matt 11:12)

It is true for those ministering as they earnestly pray for each person they are called to minister to. It is all too easy to stop a time of ministry too soon, before the healing comes. Who knows what might happen if we were prepared to give more time: *And the prayer offered in faith will make the sick person well; the Lord will raise him up.* (James 5:15)

It is also true in preparation for prayer ministry. If anyone wants to become more effective in this healing ministry they must learn the disciplines of prayer and, at times, be prepared to fast in preparation for some types, and times of ministry. (Mark 9:29 footnote).

A church which wants to see this ministry flourish should commit itself to praying that God would give them courage to keep declaring the truth that 'Our God reigns and has power to heal'. Also to asking God to perform signs and wonders amongst them: *Now, Lord, consider their threats and enable your servants to speak your word with great boldness. Stretch out your hand to heal and perform miraculous signs and wonders through the name of your holy servant Jesus. (Acts 4:29-30)*

Sometimes healing is delayed, or doesn't seem to come at all. There may be a variety of reasons for this. One is that given in the New Testament, which is applicable for anything that God wants to do, but which we don't see happening: *You want something but don't get it. ... You do not have, because you do not ask God. (James 4:2)*

A church that is committed to praying for God to release his healing power will over time see that beginning to happen. God can do it, and does do it, wherever his people ask him!

2.4 The Place of Faith

The significance of faith

Faith seems to be the purest conductor for the power of God; it brings the power of God to the point of need. On numerous occasions when Jesus heals the sick he comments on the place faith plays in creating a healing environment. Some examples are:

The woman who had been bleeding for 12 years and pushed through the crowd to touch the hem of his garment: *Just then a woman who had been subject to bleeding for twelve years came up behind him and touched the edge of his cloak. She said to herself, "If I only touch his cloak, I will be healed." Jesus turned and saw her. "Take heart, daughter," he said, "your faith has healed you." And the woman was healed from that moment.* (Matt 9:20-22)

The woman whom Jesus forgave: *Jesus said to the woman, "Your faith has saved you; go in peace."* (Luke 7:50)

One of the 10 lepers who were healed: *Then he said to him, "Rise and go; your faith has made you well."* (Luke 17:19)

Faith is important – there wasn't a single occasion when Jesus said 'Your unbelief has made you well!' Moreover, he asked on at least one occasion, whether those seeking healing believed that he could do it: *When he had gone indoors, the blind men came to him, and he asked them, "Do you believe that I am able to do this?" "Yes, Lord," they replied.* (Matt 9:28)

So we need to learn to pray the prayer: *"I do believe; help me overcome my unbelief!"* (Mark 9:24)

What does faith look like?

If we need to respond to faith as Jesus did it is important to know how to recognise faith. Interestingly it is exhibited in some very different ways. Most of us find it is easier to recognise faith expressed in some of these ways more than in others.

In some, faith is expressed very quietly and unobtrusively – such that most people, the original disciples included, would not be able to recognise it as faith. The woman who pushes her way through the crowd to touch the hem of Jesus robes is one such (Matt 9:20-22).

In some, faith is expressed noisily and exuberantly, which could be mistaken for emotionalism – as in the case of blind Bartimeaus: *When he heard that it was Jesus of Nazareth, he began to shout, "Jesus, Son of David, have mercy on me!" Many rebuked him and told him to be quiet, but he shouted all the more, "Son of David, have mercy on me!"... "What do you want me to do for you?" Jesus asked him. The blind man said, "Rabbi, I want to see." "Go," said Jesus, "your faith has healed you." Immediately he received his sight and followed Jesus along the road.* (Mark 10:47-52)

In others, faith is expressed through a type of reasoning process, easily dismissed as intellectualism. This was how the centurion's faith was expressed to Jesus: *The centurion sent friends to say to Jesus: "Lord, don't trouble yourself, for I do not deserve to have you come under my roof. That is why I did not even consider myself worthy to come to you. But say the word, and my servant will be healed. For I myself am a man under authority, with soldiers under me. I tell this one, 'Go,' and he goes; and that one, 'Come,' and he comes. I say to my servant, 'Do this,' and he does it." When Jesus heard this, he was amazed at him, and turning to the crowd following him, he said, "I tell you, I have not found such great faith even in Israel."* (Luke 7:6-9)

In others, faith is expressed through active commitment to meeting Jesus personally, even when it is difficult to do so. The faith of the friends of the paraplegic is visible through their dangerous foray onto, and then through, the roof of the house, in order to lower the stretcher at Jesus feet: *Since they could not get him to Jesus because of the crowd, they made an opening in the roof above Jesus and, after digging through it, lowered the mat the paralysed man was lying on. When Jesus saw their faith, he said to the paralytic, "Son, your sins are forgiven."* (Mark 2:4-5)

Who has to exercise faith?

On some occasions the person who comes asking for prayer is the person who is exercising faith, and whom Jesus commends – as in the case of the two blind men: *Then he touched their eyes and said, "According to your faith will it be done to you"* (Matt 9:29)

On other occasions some friend, or friends, of the suffering person are the ones who seem to have taken the initiative in coming to Jesus, and it is them that Jesus commends. One example is when the Canaanite woman comes asking for Jesus to heal her daughter: *Then Jesus answered, "Woman, you have great faith! Your request is granted." And her daughter was healed from that very hour.* (Matt 15:28)

At other times Jesus appeared to be the only one who believes that God can bring healing. At the raising of Lazarus, Martha and Mary have a vague belief that God is powerful, but it doesn't stretch to raising the dead back to life on earth. Lazarus is at this stage beyond faith! So it is left to Jesus to turn to God in faith and say: *"Take away the stone". "But, Lord," said Martha .. "by this time there is a bad odour, for he has been there four days" ...they took away the stone. Then Jesus looked up and said, "Father, I thank you that you have heard me.."..."Lazarus, come out!"...The dead man came out.* (John 11:39-44)

The faith of the person ministering

As the Lord Jesus entrusted this ministry to his disciples he said: *I tell you the truth, anyone who has faith in me will do what I have been doing. He will do even greater things than these, because I am going to the Father.* (John 14:12)

Those ministering must do all that they can to grow in their faith in Jesus. Sometimes it seems as if healing doesn't come as a result of the lack of faith of those praying: *Then the disciples came to Jesus in private and asked, "Why couldn't we drive it out?" He replied, "Because you have so little faith".* (Matt 17:19-20)

Probably it is as much the 'type' of faith rather than the 'size' of faith that is important, for Jesus continues: *"I tell you the truth, if you have faith as small as a mustard seed, you can say to this mountain, 'Move from here to there' and it will move. Nothing will be impossible for you."* (Matt 19.20)

In practise, people often have faith for different things. Some have faith for evangelism, and know they can easily lead others into the kingdom. Others have faith for money, and can easily give their money away to the poor, because they know God will always supply their needs. Others have faith for healing and are certain that, as they minister healing, the sick will be healed. God wants us to exercise faith in a number of different areas of life and ministry – not just in one of them. Moreover, we can grow and develop our faith for healing just as we can grow our faith for any of these other things.

How does faith grow?

When Paul writes to Timothy, as the leader of the church in Ephesus, he says that faith is something that should be pursued, implying that alongside other aspects of our Christian lives it can grow: *Flee the evil desires of youth, and pursue righteousness, faith, love and peace.* (2 Tim 2:22)

Faith grows:

Through hearing: *Consequently, faith comes from hearing the message, and the message is heard through the word of Christ.* (Rom 10:17)

As we read the gospel stories we see God's total commitment to healing the sick. God's character hasn't changed – he is as committed to healing today as he was then. If we immerse ourselves in the gospel accounts of what Jesus did during his physical life on earth our faith in him will grow. We can also read, listen to, and even watch on video other stories of what he is still doing – through his body, the church – around the world today. Testimonies always build faith.

Through seeing: *Believe me when I say that I am in the Father and the Father is in me; or at least believe on the evidence of the miracles themselves.* (John 14:11)

We need to deliberately go to places, churches, and conferences where the sick are being healed. 'Seeing is believing' – as we see it with our own eyes it is far easier to believe it in our hearts and spirits.

Through doing: *If a man's gift is prophesying, let him use it in proportion to his faith.* (Rom 12:6)

We don't need to have a lot of faith to start using the spiritual gifts, and ministering healing. God has 'hidden these things from the wise and learned, and revealed them to little children' (Luke 10.21). Just as a muscle is strengthened and grows through use, so too does our faith. But just as a muscle atrophies through lack of use, faith can wither if we don't exercise it. Consequently Paul instructs these Christians to keep exercising their faith and keep prophesying.

Through persevering in difficult times: *Let us fix our eyes on Jesus, the author and perfecter of our faith. (Heb 12:2)*

Just as Jesus brings us to faith in the first place, he is also committed to growing our faith within us. This growth sometimes comes through difficulties in our lives. These trials, or tests, of our faith are sent by God to refine and develop our faith: *These (trials) have come so that your faith-of greater worth than gold, which perishes even though refined by fire-may be proved genuine and may result in praise, glory and honour when Jesus Christ is revealed. (1 Pet 1:7)*

Most individuals and churches that start to minister healing do not find the learning process easy, or unopposed. God uses these difficult times to test our determination to become more like Jesus in this, as in every other aspect, of ministry.

To become more effective those involved in ministering healing need to keep growing their experience and faith in God in these different ways.

The faith environment

On three occasions in the gospels it appears as if an unbelieving environment can exercise a restraining power over the working of signs and wonders.

When a father brings his demonised boy to the disciples for healing they are unable to set him free. When Jesus rejoins them, on his return from the Mount of Transfiguration he says: *"O unbelieving and perverse generation," Jesus replied, "how long shall I stay with you? How long shall I put up with you?" (Matt 17:17)*

When Jesus is visiting his home town and it appears as if he is unable to work miracles there as freely as elsewhere. The explanation given is the lack of faith of those there: *He could not do any miracles there, except lay his hands on a few sick people and heal them. And he was amazed at their lack of faith. (Mark 6:5-6)*

When a blind man is brought to him in Bethsaida Jesus takes him out of town to heal him, and then warns him not to go home through Bethsaida (Mark 8.22-26). The reason seems to be that the town had been given the opportunity to respond to the gospel but had instead hardened their hearts. (Luke 10.13-14). Jesus was aware that their hardness to the gospel could make the village a difficult place in which to heal or be healed.

In our day a whole nation can be affected by the predominant attitude of its leader or opinion formers. In cultures around the world where there is a ready understanding of, and belief in, the supernatural – in Singapore for example it seems that local churches find it relatively easy to engage in effective healing ministry. In contrast, in the Western world, dominated until recently by a scientific rational world view – in which the supernatural has so often been scorned – it is relatively difficult to start teaching and practising this ministry.

The history of a particular nation, or local church, can also have a big impact on the present population or congregation. Church leaders therefore need to be sensitive to this history. They also need to be careful that in their preaching, and in the way they live their lives, they are imparting faith, rather than doubt to their church members.

Having said all this we know of various cases where people have been healed while they had little or no faith – either before or after they were healed. Similarly, those ministering may think they have had little or no faith. God is sovereign, and he is able to heal whomever, and whenever, he chooses. We will often be surprised by his amazing grace!

Conclusion

All these values operate like lighthouses. If we keep focused on these, and trust in God, we shall avoid shipwrecks in this ministry.

3 SPECIFIC TYPES OF MINISTRY

3.1 Leading Someone to Christ

In your interview, seek to discern what the person is responding to. Verify if this is a first time commitment or the latest of many. If the latter, it may be that what is needed is a scriptural basis for assurance and/or release of the Holy Spirit in their lives. Ascertain if the person is just being moved emotionally, with little understanding of what receiving Christ means, or has come to this decision to give their life to Christ after some time of thinking and preparation.

There is no fixed formula for leading a person to Christ. Be open to the leading of the Spirit, and listen and respond carefully to what the person is saying. It is helpful to keep in mind some basic stepping stones as you lead a person in prayer, but don't be bound by the order.

For a person to commit their life to Jesus Christ they normally have to be ready to do a number of things. Here is a simple ABCD approach, which can be a helpful guideline:

Admit their need

Ultimately this is the need of forgiveness from a Holy God who is ultimately our judge.
For all have sinned and fall short of the glory of God, (Rom 3:23)
For the wages of sin is death (Rom 6:23)

Sin is universal, it has spoilt us and separated us from God; the chasm is so great that it cannot be bridged from man's side.

Sometimes a person may not be very articulate about this need of forgiveness; but the Holy Spirit has made them aware that 'something' is missing, and that it can be found in Jesus.

Believe in Christ

God is longing to bring us back into the loving relationship with him for which he created us. He does this through sending his Son Jesus to take our sin and all its consequences in our place: *"God so loved the world (i.e. us) that He gave His one and only Son that whoever believes in Him shall not perish but have eternal life."* (John 3:16)

For Christ died for sins, once for all, the righteous for the unrighteous, to bring you to God. (1 Peter 3:18)

Some people may not be really aware that only Jesus could do, and has done this; but over time the Holy Spirit is able to bring someone to the awareness of his uniqueness.

Commit, confess, change

Committing one's life to Christ must involve the confessing and renouncing of all known sin, and the willingness to commit to a lifetime of allowing God to change us from the inside out by his Holy Spirit: *Jesus said to them all, "If anyone would come after me, he must deny himself and take up his cross daily and follow me. For whoever wants to save his life will lose it, but whoever loses his life for me will save it."* (Luke 9:23-24)

It doesn't matter how relatively good or sinful a life a person has lived up to this point; the issue is their willingness to admit they have been living the wrong way without Jesus, and their willingness to change direction, call on his help and be changed from now on.

Declare their faith to others

In the New Testament there is no such thing as a secret believer. Normally new believers were immediately publicly baptised, joined the church, and then required to bear witness for their faith: *If you confess with your mouth, "Jesus is Lord," and believe in your heart that God raised him from the dead, you will be saved.* (Rom 10:9)

If a person is willing to become known as a Christian immediately it usually means they are now ready and serious about giving their life to Christ. If they are not willing they may not be ready.

One way of leading a person through this process is by asking them such questions as these:

Do you realise your need of Jesus?

Do you believe that God loves you so much that he has done everything to forgive you and save you by sending Jesus to die and rise again for you?

Do you realise that Jesus would have done this for you had you been the only sinner alive in the world?

Are you willing to confess your sin, and have your life changed?

Are you willing to be known as a Christian?

If they answer yes, tell them God is wanting them to give their life to Christ right now. The only question is would they like to do so?

Prayer

Ask if you can pray a prayer with them. Ask them to confess their sin in a simple prayer, to declare their belief in Jesus, to ask him to come into their life by his Holy Spirit, and to ask him to change them and help them to live as a Christian for the rest of their life.

Some people may be able to articulate this prayer for themselves. For others you may need to pray it aloud, sentence by sentence, asking them to repeat each phrase after you. Some may take time over different parts, depending on the extent of the convicting work of the Spirit.

If a person does make this response, then thank the Lord Jesus that he has now come into the person's life, and that Jesus has promised that he will never leave them.

Filling with the Holy Spirit

Finish by asking if you can pray for them to be filled with the Spirit, to know the joy of having Jesus in their life, and to be strengthened to live for him every day. If they consent, gently lay hands on them and ask the Holy Spirit to fill them. Pray silently in tongues over them. Aloud ask God to give them more of His Spirit of righteousness, joy and peace. If the new Christian is obviously responding to the coming of the Holy Spirit you may feel it appropriate to encourage them to pray in tongues as well. The sooner they do this the better.

Follow Up

This may depend upon whether you are in your home church, at a conference, or in a faith-sharing situation. It is generally very helpful to share some of your own testimony – how you follow Jesus Christ in your prayer life, in reading the Scriptures, and in the fellowship and service to others in a local church.

Introduce them to the idea of reading the Scriptures for themselves so that they can see that these things are true. You could for instance give them Mark's Gospel and describe the best way of reading it. If you can give them a booklet such as 'Why Jesus?' this will also help them to become assured in the prayer and decision they have made.

It is also a good idea to say a little about the spiritual battle (temptation, etc.) and the way to overcome any doubts that the enemy might throw at them over the next few days. Don't overdo this, but a little warning is very helpful.

Encourage the new Christian to make contact with a local church and even to get in touch with a church minister. The minister should be able to introduce these new converts to some kind of beginners' group – such as an Alpha Course, etc.

3.2 Ministering Forgiveness

Many Christians spend years of their Christian lives harbouring secret feelings of shame and guilt which gnaw away at their spiritual vitality, and make them relatively ineffective as Christians. If this is as a result of their own sin they need to know the reality of God's forgiveness. If this is as a result of sin against them they need to experience release from that trauma, and from any unforgiveness they are holding towards the perpetrator of that sin. This area of healing, sometimes called inner healing, is all about the appropriation of the forgiveness of Jesus.

Helping someone receive forgiveness

Sometimes people need to confess their sin to the Lord in front of others, in order to receive their healing from past shame: *Therefore confess your sins to each other and pray for each other so that you may be healed. (James 5:16)*

Some people may be willing to do this aloud, others may be too embarrassed to do so. We need to give them space to make a silent confession. At the same time we encourage them to renounce these sinful practises in the future.

When they have finished praying we use the authority that we have been given to minister forgiveness in the name of Jesus: *If you forgive anyone his sins, they are forgiven; if you do not forgive them, they are not forgiven. (John 20:23)*

It can sometimes be helpful to:

Declare Scripture over the person, for instance: *God says 'If we confess our sins, he is faithful and just and will forgive us our sins and purify us from all unrighteousness.' (1 John 1:9)*

Proclaim forgiveness: 'As a servant of Jesus I proclaim that whatever you have confessed is now forgiven by the blood of Jesus.'

Pronounce a cleansing with Jesus' blood: 'I pour the blood of Jesus over you (or a part of the body that has been involved in the sin), which cleanses you from all sin, and washes whiter than snow.'

Sign with the cross: 'I sign you with the cross as an assurance that whatever you have confessed is now forgiven by the blood of Jesus on the cross.'

Always give the Holy Spirit time to take the words and apply them to the person's spirit, and the person time to enjoy the experience of having their inner spirit cleansed from the sin, shame, and accusation of the enemy.

If a person has confessed sin and received the assurance of their forgiveness it is good to help them to know how to avoid that temptation again.

Finish this time with a prayer of thanks, and a prayer consecrating every affected part of the person's life back to the Lord. This offering of the parts of the body can be especially freeing when sexual sin has been involved. It is an application of offering ourselves to the Lord, and thereby having the joy of knowing God's way is the best way for them in the future: *Therefore, I urge you, brothers, in view of God's mercy, to offer your bodies as living sacrifices, holy and pleasing to God – this is your spiritual act of worship. Do not conform any longer to the pattern of this world, but be transformed by the renewing of your mind. Then you will be able to test and approve what God's will is – his good, pleasing and perfect will. (Rom 12:1-2)*

Helping someone release forgiveness

When we have been sinned against, and are traumatised by that experience, it is very easy to build resentment, anger, and unforgiveness towards the person who has done this. We can become so tormented by this that every area of our lives can be effected, and we become the victim of the enemy.

Forgiveness means that we stop feeling resentment against someone who has hurt us, and we cancel a person's record with us and transfer the responsibility for any punishment of them to God.

In ministering this freedom we may need to gently point out why it is so necessary to forgive. Because:

In Christ God forgave us and restored our relationship with Him (Eph 4:32)

Unless we forgive we will struggle to experience forgiveness (Matt 6:15)

Forgiveness releases from the past, restores the present, and heals for the future

Forgiveness enables us to empty our hearts of hatred.

Forgiveness opens us to Christ's power to be healed.

In prayer we need to take a person through a number of steps. The order here is often significant. It is sometimes tempting to jump ahead before the person is ready to take that step. Be patient in leading someone down this road.

1. Ask God (by His Holy Spirit) to show you together the root cause of the hurt.

2. Allow the person to describe the trauma, and then to express to God the pain of the hurt. This may involve them reliving the moment, and involve strong emotion – including crying, wailing, or anger.

3. When they are ready, ask the person to resolve (be willing) to forgive the perpetrator for the action and the attitude that caused the hurt.

4. Bring them to the point where they can ask God to forgive the perpetrator for causing the hurt. (Sometimes it is not possible to move from 3 to 4 in one prayer session. It may take some time, weeks or months, before they are able to ask God to forgive rather than judge the person. Don't push a person to do this before they are ready – the Holy Spirit will bring the willing person to this point at some stage.)

5. Now ask them to ask God to forgive them for the sins of bitterness, anger, resentment etc. that they have held on to.

6. Get them to bless aloud the perpetrator by name. Encourage them to do that silently whenever they think of the perpetrator again – even in their absence.

7. Ask the Holy Spirit to come, to heal the hurt, and to fill them with new hope for a life free from this unforgiveness and its consequences.

This process is one that we can lead a person through even if the perpetrator is dead. The point about unforgiveness is that it binds and harms the person unwilling to forgive, not the perpetrator who often is either unaware of the pain they have caused, or has too hard a conscience to be troubled by their sin. So the death of the perpetrator doesn't release the hurting person.

This is the kingdom ministry that Jesus intends his church to have: *I will give you the keys of the kingdom of heaven; whatever you bind on earth will be bound in heaven, and whatever you loose on earth will be loosed in heaven.* (Matt 16:19)

Conclusion

In ministering forgiveness we need to remain unshockable, patient and merciful. The guile and the depravity of the enemy know no bounds. We will find ourselves needing to listen and respond with great grace to those who have become victims of the enemy in this way.

3.3 Filling with the Holy Spirit

We will often be ministering to born-again Christians who want to be filled anew with the Holy Spirit. In your initial contact seek to discover if there are any obvious barriers preventing the person from experiencing the fullness of the Holy Spirit.

Possible Barriers

Ignorance

The person may be like those in Ephesus who, when Paul asked them if they had received the Holy Spirit, replied *"We have not ever heard that there is a Holy Spirit"* (Acts 19:2). Although they may have heard about the Holy Spirit theologically, they may never have been told that he wants to fill and irradiate their lives with assurance, joy, peace in believing, and power to live and be a witness for Jesus. So many long for this but don't realise it is the filling of the Holy Spirit that leads them into this full appreciation of their birth-right as Christians.

Speak about God's longing to give his Holy Spirit to all those who ask. Read and explain such Bible passages as: *And afterward, I will pour out my Spirit on all people. Your sons and daughters will prophesy, your old men will dream dreams, your young men will see visions. Even on my servants, both men and women, I will pour out my Spirit in those days.* (Joel 2:28-9)

Peter replied, "Repent and be baptised, every one of you, in the name of Jesus Christ for the forgiveness of your sins. And you will receive the gift of the Holy Spirit. The promise is for you and your children and for all who are far off – for all whom the Lord our God will call." (Acts 2:38-39)

If you then, though you are evil, know how to give good gifts to your children, how much more will your Father in heaven give the Holy Spirit to those who ask him! (Luke 11:13)

The common theme in all these passages is God's willingness to give to all who ask, whatever their age, sex, or background.

Hostility and Fear

These often revolve around a person's negative experiences of authority figures. They transfer these experiences onto God and consequently are uncertain or uncomfortable with the thought of a close relationship with him. It is quite common to find real fear over what God might do to the person if they were to open themselves completely to the Holy Spirit, become intimate with Him, and let Him be Lord over every aspect of their life.

If this is the case reassure the person of the unconditional nature of God's love. Read and explain appropriate Scriptures such as: *And so we know and rely on the love God has for us. God is love.* (1 John 4:16)

" I know the plans I have for you," declares the LORD, "plans to prosper you and not to harm you, plans to give you hope and a future." (Jer 29:11) See also 1 John 4:9-21

Spiritual and Moral Barriers

Sometimes at conferences people come forward asking to be filled with the Spirit before they have really made a commitment to Christ. Sensitively enquire whether they have done so, and if not, take them through a prayer of commitment as outlined in 3.1 above.

A person may be holding 'unforgiveness' in their heart. If so it may be important to help them release forgiveness (along the lines of 3.2 above). However sometimes a fresh filling with the Spirit of love helps someone to release and/or receive true forgiveness.

A person may have been involved in 'spiritually grey areas' which, although they may have seemed harmless enough at the time, are known as 'occult'. There may have been consultation with fortune-tellers, palm readers, ouija boards, horoscopes, etc. These things are spiritually dangerous, often damaging, and lead to spiritual oppression in our lives. This is why God says: *Let no one be found among you who sacrifices his son or daughter in the fire, who practices divination or sorcery, interprets omens, engages in witchcraft,* (Deut 18:10)

A person may be, or has been, living in some sort of immoral relationship, or engaging in immoral practises of one sort or another. They will need to confess, repent, and be forgiven (see 3.2 above). A person may be full of 'unbelief' as a result of false teaching in the past, or through negative experiences of Pentecostal ministry. If so, they need to acknowledge this and pray a prayer such as: *"I do believe; help me overcome my unbelief!"* (Mark 9:24)

Filling with the Spirit

Preparation

Depending on the circumstances, this could involve:

Confession of sin; Renouncing involvement in demonic activity; Forgiving those who have been hurtful; Renouncing a wrong relationship.

It may be necessary at this stage to speak forgiveness in Jesus' name, and/or cut the person free in areas of bondage through Jesus' name.

Explain that the Spirit does not come without his gifts. Ask if they want, and are willing, to be released into the gifts of the Spirit, even the gift of tongues. This is an obviously supernatural gift, and some are frightened of receiving it. To want to receive it is one sign of a willingness to make the Holy Spirit the Lord of their whole life, rather than just a visitor in the guest room. On the other hand to be unwilling to receive this gift is sometimes a sign of an unwillingness to be really filled to overflowing with the Spirit.

Explain about how wonderful the gift of tongues is for everyone who wants to be drawn closer to God in prayer, and be built up in their faith: *For anyone who speaks in a tongue does not speak to men but to God... he utters mysteries with his spirit.* (1 Cor:14:1-4)

Having said this we know that many who have been filled with the Holy Spirit have not yet spoken in tongues, even though we believe that they could easily do so.

Receiving the filling

This may take a little time – it is not a case of waving a magic wand! It is a case of giving God time to fill one of his children with an overwhelming, and overflowing, awareness of his presence, his love, his peace and his power.

Encourage the person to ask Jesus to fill them with his Spirit. Lay hands on them in an appropriate way, and pray quietly for Jesus to fill them with his Spirit. At the same time invite them to be open and welcoming of the Holy Spirit.

Be sensitive to any prophetic words the Spirit gives you for the person being prayed for. This can build up faith, and help people to open up further to the filling of the Spirit.

Watch for manifestations of the Spirit's presence and bless all that he is doing. Get them to express their thanks to Jesus for filling them with his Spirit and for what he is doing in their life right now.

Ask them whether they would like to speak in tongues. Explain that often it will seem as if they are making it up and that it will not feel like a language, but just strange sounds. Explain that any young child learns language in this way, and moves to form a vocabulary, syntax, and grammar over a period of time.

Now pray quietly alongside them in tongues, and ask God to release this gift in them. If necessary pray for God to release their throat, their mouth, and their tongue. And maybe, with a hand on their stomach, pray for God to release the *'streams of living water... from within him'.* (John 7:38)

Encourage them to 'have a go'. As they begin to speak in their new language encourage them that this really is God's gift to them.

Conclusion

Give people the opportunity to ask questions about what has just happened. If there have been any prophetic words write them down and encourage them to pray over them in the days ahead.

Encourage the use of tongues daily in their personal prayer time. Remind them that the gift is theirs to use, or not, whenever they choose to pray like that: *So what shall I do? I will pray with my spirit, but I will also pray with my mind; I will sing with my spirit, but I will also sing with my mind.* (1 Cor 14:15)

Tell them they can also use the gift during sung worship in public meetings. This can be a good place to 'practise', and get familiar with the sound of one's own voice speaking another language.

Remind them that the enemy does not want to see God's children being equipped with the power tools of the Holy Spirit with which to oppose him, and will be tempting the recent recipient to give up, insinuating 'it is all rubbish'.

3.4 Ministering Deliverance

The ministry of deliverance – or the healing of the oppressed – is part of Christ's commission to his disciples (Luke 9:1). So deliverance is an integral part of Christian ministry to individuals today. There is no need to be frightened of, or even impressed, by demons. We serve the Lord of the Universe, to whom *"All authority in heaven and on earth has been given to me"* (Matt 28.18), so there is no question of who is stronger. Moreover we can rest assured of his protection when we are involved in this ministry because: *The one who is in you is greater than the one who is in the world.* (1 John 4:4)

What are demons?

They are evil spirits, agents of the enemy, who seek to trouble and destroy some aspect of our life or personality. The authorised version of the Bible often refers to them as 'unclean'. In Jesus' ministry we see him dealing with demons which have brought sickness, such as blindness, dumbness, or epilepsy, and acute physical aggression.

Jesus did not develop a demonology, though he does reveal to us quite a lot about the devil himself. It is clear from the rest of the New Testament that there are a variety of evil forces under a unified head, the devil himself. Jesus' main concern was to cast out demons from those afflicted by them, so that they could enjoy life as God intends it to be. Our main concern ought to be the same, rather than the building of a speculative demonology, based on minimal biblical evidence.

In the gospels there are clearly different degrees of oppression. Some are described simply; Those troubled by evil spirits (Luke 6:18) – they were cured. Others are more clearly possessed, as in the case of the man who lived in the graveyard (Mark 5). Generally, because of the stigma attached with this, it is more helpful to talk about being 'demonised' than demon-possessed. 'Demonised' can then used in the same way we use the word 'sick' in England. If we describe someone as 'sick' it may be anything ranging from a headache to a long-term life threatening illness.

How do they gain access?

They can gain access whenever people are in some way involved in spiritual rebellion against God. This is what the devil did, when as an angel, created by God, he became proud and rebelled. He involved other angels in that rebellion, who are now his demons. When the human race fell, through temptation by the devil, the human race became involved in that rebellion. When individual human beings become deliberately rebellious against God they open themselves up to demonistation.

There are a number of common entry points, or footholds:

Deliberate sin and uncontrolled emotions

In your anger do not sin: Do not let the sun go down while you are still angry, and do not give the devil a foothold. (Eph 4:26-7)

Uncontrolled anger is not the only type of habitual sin that gives the devil a foothold. Alcoholism, drug abuse, hatred, violence, abuse of power and privilege are others. Emotional traumas, strong negative attitudes resulting from past hurts or deprivations, and wilful unforgiveness are also commonly used by the devil to bring his oppression into people's lives.

Sexual immorality

Flee from sexual immorality. All other sins a man commits are outside his body, but he who sins sexually sins against his own body. Do you not know that your body is a temple of the Holy Spirit, who is in you, whom you have received from God? You are not your own. (1 Cor 6:18-19)

Paul is suggesting that if we are involved in sexual immorality we are opening our bodies up to be the 'temple' for other spirits – rather than the Holy Spirit.

False worship of other gods

You belong to your father, the devil, and you want to carry out your father's desire. ... When he lies, he speaks his native language, for he is a liar and the father of lies. (John 8:44)

Involvement in worship which steadfastly denies that Jesus is the Christ – especially occult practices, seances, ouija boards, witchcraft and the like – open people up to a control from the enemy, because they are based on the ultimate lie; namely that Jesus is not the unique Son through whom alone we can both approach God and be restored to a relationship with him.

Inheritance

You shall not bow down to them or worship them; for I, the LORD your God, am a jealous God, punishing the children for the sin of the fathers to the third and fourth generation of those who hate me. (Exod 20:5)

Sometimes people become demonised via a parent, or as a result of a covenant with the devil entered into on their part by a parent or guardian.

Indications of an evil spirit's presence

Common indications are:

Discernment or revelation from the Holy Spirit. This needs careful checking. It is unwise ever to suggest to someone they are demonised. In the end demons will normally reveal themselves through other 'symptoms'.

Manifestation of a power 'encounter' in worship, or when the Spirit comes in power in a meeting. This may be convulsive reaction to the presence of the Spirit of God as he comes to deliver; but great care is needed because people can also respond to the anointing of God with strange manifestations.

When being prayed for there may be:

More violent physical response to the name of Jesus, or the blood of the cross.

Pain moving about in their body, or eyes rolling back in their sockets.

A 'spirit' speaking within, so the person is hearing voices.

A different voice speaking out aloud through the person.

Disengagement from the ministry with sleepiness, inertness, or 'death like' symptoms

So one way to begin to discern whether a spirit is present is to begin with a prayer such as 'I shine the light of Jesus into any dark places in your life', or 'I bring you to the foot of the cross where Jesus shed his blood for you'; then wait and see how the person responds as the Holy Spirit takes your words into the person's spirit.

A dread of going into any place with a strong Christian association (i.e. a Church), or shouting out in worship, or blaspheming at the mention of the name of Jesus or the blood of Jesus shed on the cross.

Yielding to compulsive desires which are clearly out of control, including self-mutilation, self-destructive tendencies, and active destructive and aggressive attitudes towards others.

Some of the 'apparent symptoms' of oppression could be signs of the Holy Spirit touching deep hurts and not necessarily evidence of demonic activity at all. Additionally an anointing for prophecy or intercession can also be accompanied by strange contortions and noise, so great care is needed in discernment.

Guidelines for Ministry

If during general ministry you come across the need for deliverance you can often do this relatively silently and quickly. However should there be no adequate conclusion to the ministry it is best, in consultation with the church leadership, to deliberately plan a convenient time for further ministry. It is not always necessary to deal with it immediately.

Be careful about choosing the time for ministry. A suitable appointment during daylight is often better than dealing with this late at night. Make sure it is at a time others can join you. It is unwise to minister on your own.

Prepare yourself before a planned ministry time; confess sins, seek fresh anointing of the Holy Spirit and put on the whole armour of God. Sometimes a time of prayer and fasting beforehand can speed up deliverance.

Check whether the individual is under medical supervision, taking medication or has a history of mental illness. Demonic oppression may not be the most serious problem the person has – long-term traumatised emotions may be more problematic. If so, it is important that deliverance ministry should be part of the healing process that has already begun, rather than overrule or arrest this.

It is unwise ever to suggest to someone that they have an evil spirit until you have checked it out with others in the church's leadership. When you are reasonably sure this is the case, minister in mixed groups of 3 or 4 for any significant ministry. There should be at least one person of the same sex as the person being prayed for present. Do not allow bystanders to congregate – the devil loves drawing attention to his work. Jesus sometimes drew people aside to minister privately to them.

Encourage the person to be relaxed and to focus on Jesus. Invite the Holy Spirit to come – and hereafter listen to the Lord and 'track' what the Spirit is doing. Remember that at any time in the course of ministry you can stop and talk. The agreement and co-operation of the person is usually vital. They will also often be able to discern and talk about what is happening inside them. Sometimes people fail to co-operate because they sense the demon's fear and think it's theirs, or they feel they will lose something of their identity if the demon were to leave.

Treat the person the way you would like to be treated yourself if you were the one being ministered to. So offer any 'words of knowledge' sensitively. Always remember you could be wrong. Similarly try to find words which do not imply guilt.

Tell the person that during the ministry you will sometimes be addressing the spirit, and sometimes be talking to them. Assure them of God's infinite love for them, his hatred of the enemy and all that the enemy has done to them, and his ability and longing to free them.

Don't allow excessive manifestations. Rebuke or bind the evil spirit in the name of Jesus. If the demon is apparently in total control (sometimes with the help of drink or drugs), and you are unable to get through to the real person, then do not persist in ministry. Let the afflicted person sleep it off and return to the ministry at a suitable date later.

It is sometimes taught that you need to know the demon's name. It might be revealed in the process of dialogue. Although this is supposed to be a help, the demon itself is not likely to give its own name away readily and even if it did it could not be trusted anyway because demons come from the father of lies! It is best to dialogue as little as possible with demons. Jesus commanded them to 'be quiet' (Mark 1.25).

Do demons come in clusters? This is often taught, but should never be assumed. It is best to allow plenty of time after an expulsion of a demon. An afflicted person (usually very keen to get delivered) may well continue to exhibit symptoms of demonisation if they think you believe there are still others there. We are all very susceptible to suggestion.

The person receiving ministry needs to take responsibility and deal with their own sin, repenting where necessary and as the Spirit leads. Similarly, hurts, traumas, and anything inherited, need to be acknowledged and renounced, asking for God's help where needed. Often oppression lifts at this stage even without 'formal expulsion'.

At an appropriate moment address the demon directly in Jesus' name and command it to go. Looking straight into the eyes whilst doing this can help. Advise the person to co-operate fully by putting their will into this. There is no point in continuing if the person will not co-operate in this way.

If there is no response to a firm command, ask the Holy Spirit for guidance. Remember it's the power of God which shifts demons, not you – so shouting won't help! If in doubt, or you come to a blockage, delay rather than labour on.

Check with the person whether the oppression seems to have gone. They will normally be aware of an inner struggle during deliverance, and will know when they are freed.

Once the person is delivered pray for their infilling with the Holy Spirit and give glory to God.

Always finish by praying for the peace of God to fill them.

Follow Up

Recognise that the person will need ongoing support. Encourage the person to contact you again if needed. In any case try to contact them within the next 48 hours if at all possible. Sometimes people are left physically, emotionally, and spiritually exhausted in the immediate aftermath of deliverance. They may need to rest and relax in order to recover. Their continuing healing from the trauma of what the enemy has done to them will come as they learn to stand in their healing, worship God in spirit and truth, receive communion, enjoy being a part of a healing community – which the church is meant to be – and belong to a small accountability group, like a home-group.

3.5 Pastoral Prayer Ministry

Pastoral Prayer Ministry (PPM) is an on-going ministry to deeper needs – often of an emotional and psychological nature. Almost as soon as healing prayer ministry is offered in most churches it is apparent that some people's needs have not been adequately addressed during after-service prayer ministry. Some provision for dealing with these needs on a planned basis over a longer period of time is helpful if the local church is to become the healing community that God really intends it to be. A team will need to be trained and deployed under a wisely appointed, and suitably equipped, team leader.

Levels of Need

Our churches are full of people with little understanding about where their own responsibility lies for their healing and growth, and where other Christians, empowered by the Spirit can help them. God has placed us in the community of the church so that we can help each other to grow to maturity: *Carry each other's burdens, and in this way you will fulfil the law of Christ. (Gal 6:2)*

At the same time we should learn to stand on our own two feet: *Each one should carry his own load. (Gal 6:5)*

In a healthy church many people will find measures of healing from all sorts of emotional traumas as they engage in Spirit-filled worship, as they seek the Lord through the Scriptures, and as they avail themselves of the victory of Jesus on the cross.

But another God-given way of receiving healing is through the prayer of fellow-believers: *Therefore confess your sins to each other and pray for each other so that you may be healed. (James 5:16)*

Some of this confession, prayer and healing should be happening during the regular after-service prayer ministry. This may occur on a one-off occasion, or over a period of 3-4 weeks, during which time an individual seeks prayer weekly. Some of it may also be happening in an effective wholistic small group, in which people can be open and honest about their lives, and receive prayer ministry.

However there are some who have experienced deep hurt and emotional trauma, often as a result of dysfunctional family backgrounds, who need longer term help. Similarly, there are others who have made such wrong choices, and fallen into sin so deeply, that they are now trapped in irrational beliefs and behaviour patterns which are destroying their lives. These people too may need longer term prayer ministry.

We recommend that this PPM is only offered to members of the church who are involved in its wider life though worship, prayer, teaching, serving and fellowship. These things help a person to continue to receive healing through a variety of means between the ministry appointments.

Guidelines

If a church is to offer help there are some essential steps to be put in place.

This sort of ministry requires a certain amount of experience and time. A church needs to know whether it has people who have that wisdom and experience, and who are willing to give time to this ministry. Good training can complement experience, but this involves time too! It helps if everyone in this ministry is involved in the after-service ministry where they can regularly see God at work through his Holy Spirit.

Some sort of 'assessing' process needs to be put in place. This should be done by someone who will be able to discern whether the person seeking help comes within the scope of the abilities of the PPM team. Knowing our limitations, as well as the power of the Lord to heal, is important if we are to exercise this ministry well.

As with all other types of ministry it should not be undertaken alone, but in pairs, always using someone of the same sex as the individual coming for ministry. There should be a deep spiritual harmony between those ministering. Because this involves working very closely together, we do not recommend that anyone work in partnership with someone of the opposite sex – apart from their spouse.

We recommend an initial commitment to 4-6 sessions. Then it should be reviewed before you offer any further commitment. This sort of time limitation also encourages a person to focus their energy on making progress during the period. It gives both sides a chance to review the effectiveness of the ministry, and those ministering the opportunity to stop the ministry if they feel it is not being profitable.

The availability of a prayer room within the church building is to be preferred over the use of the home. This helps both those ministering, and the one receiving ministry, to conduct this PPM in a planned and relatively business-like manner, to maintain some necessary boundaries, and to avoid any possible over-dependency developing. A session should be limited in length – normally 90 minutes maximum – since this is an emotionally, spiritually, and sometimes physically, draining ministry for everyone.

The willingness and co-operation of the person seeking prayer is vital. Apart from co-operating during the ministry time they may need to engage in the keeping of a prayer journal, the reading of prescribed scriptures and recommended Christian books, as well as the setting of some other interim goals to speed their healing. Outlining this clearly creates greater commitment to the exercise. In some cases, when ministry is difficult and there is no quick and easy resolution, reference back to this commitment can break the logjam.

Brief notes should be maintained by the prayer couple. These should not be held centrally or copied. They must be kept absolutely confidential. The keeping of notes enables everyone to see what issues have been dealt with and what progress has been made.

We always value professional help and are quite willing to advise an individual to seek professional support when this is needed. If there is any doubt, with the individual's permission and the church leader's approval, the individual's doctor can be consulted. If the person is on medication this is especially important before engaging in prolonged PPM.

If there is a local Christian doctor or psychiatrist they could be enlisted to act as a long-stop, or reference point, for the church or PPM team leader. This can create a degree of safety both for those seeking and those giving ministry.

Conclusion

God is all powerful; he can and does wonderful work in bringing healing to all sorts of traumatised people through the prayers of Christians who are open to the guidance and power of the Holy Spirit. However it is not possible to 'run before learning to walk'. Initiating, establishing and then developing this PPM is a long term commitment that requires wisdom, energy, and perseverance. Keeping in close touch with other churches on the same learning curve can prove really helpful.

4 ARENAS OF MINISTRY

4.1 In the Local Church

The natural place for healing ministry is in, and through, the local church congregation. God gives gifts of healing from the Holy Spirit because he intends the people of God to become known as a healing community. This booklet has regularly made this assumption.

It is up to every church leader to determine to follow the lead of the Spirit, and courageously establish a healing ministry in their church. Some religious people may oppose it; they did in Jesus day, and he said we were to expect the same: *It is enough for the student to be like his teacher, and the servant like his master. If the head of the house has been called Beelzebub, how much more the members of his household!* (Matt 10:25)

As we begin to introduce this ministry we may find that 'It won't be long before they call your good evil'. (David Pytches).

Some may reject the church's healing ministry, and us too (Matt 10.14), but others will welcome it. In an age of alternative medicine, and increasing openness to any type of spirituality which transcends the purely rational, this is happening more and more.

The Church Leader's Role

If this ministry is to have credibility and be effective it must be owned by the overall church leader. That person must believe in it, initiate it and take responsibility for seeing it develop. In practise they can not be closely involved in the prayer ministry – if they were to be so it would draw them away from their other responsibilities and duties as the church leader. It is a time consuming ministry.

The overall church leader can encourage this ministry and exercise leadership of it by:

Teaching

The whole church needs good biblical-based teaching on the need to face up to life's hurts, on how to receive God's healing for them, and on the work of the Holy Spirit in leading us into wholeness in Christ. This will bring a constant supply of people seeking this ministry. The whole healing ministry team needs to be trained and supported, if not always by the leader directly, then by the provision for good training by others who share their values. Those involved in Pastoral Prayer Ministry will need additional and ongoing training, supervision and encouragement.

Delegation

Leaders may be in danger of falling into two traps. First they may over-delegate to the point of non-involvement, in which case the ministry will probably either die through lack of support, or come into disrepute through lack of accountability. Second they may be over-involved, resulting either in over-control and a failure to release the gifting of others, or in a withering of this ministry due to neglect through inadequate time being given to it in the leader's busy schedule.

Creating a 'safe place'

Getting in touch with repressed emotions is never entirely safe. People will never do that unless they feel they are in a 'safe place'. Lack of confidentiality, obvious expression of shock over sin, and accusations of guilt, are sure to make a church feel an unsafe place. A leader who is known and seen to be open, vulnerable, self-disclosing, and in accountable relationships within the church, can help to create a 'safe place' for others. This can be done both through teaching and example.

Authorisation

Those who are appointed to be the leaders of this ministry must carry the complete trust of the overall church leader. At the same time they should be held in high regard by members of the church. This is an exposed position of high responsibility, and those appointed should be known for their humility, purity, and integrity, as well as being full of faith and the Holy Spirit. They must be willing to exercise this ministry under the authority of the leader. The church leader must be happy with others who are appointed to the team. Their decision must be allowed to overrule the opinion of the ministry team leader. The overall church leader is in the end accountable to God for the wise exercising of this ministry.

Resolving Difficulties

Should there be any report or concern expressed by someone who has received inappropriate ministry in the church, the leader will need to deal with it straight away. They may choose to do this through the ministry team leader in the first instance, but ultimately they may have to get involved. If there is something definite to act on, then the team member concerned may need to be placed alongside someone more experienced, and be reminded of the values undergirding this ministry. In some cases a person may need to be 'stood down' for a while, especially if they are unwilling to receive this discipline, or if they need to give attention to difficult issues in their own life. The way the church leader handles this kind of issue is important for the long term credibility of the ministry.

In our experience, if this ministry is to flourish in a church then the leader must be involved to some degree. Most church leaders find it hard to permit things in their churches that they don't really believe in or feel 'at ease' with. This is because they have to give an account to God of their oversight of the church, and good leaders can not take that lightly.

If you are reading this as a church member, and your leader is not yet ready to introduce such a ministry publicly, there are a number of things you can do – following our guidelines. First, take every opportunity you can to minister healing to people in your home, and as you meet people in the normal course of your life. Second, continue to love and pray for your leader(s). Gently encourage them with stories of what God has been doing as you have ministered to people elsewhere. Third, try to take your leader with you to some event that will enable them to see God at work in a way which you think they may be able to learn about it and accept it. (A 'wild' Pentecostal/charismatic meeting may not be the easiest learning place for an average Anglican Vicar!) Fourth, if they give you permission to develop something publicly as part of the church's ministry always keep open and honest lines of communication with them. Go at the pace they are allowing you to go – even if this is slower than you might like.

Introducing this Ministry

When Jesus sent out the disciples into the villages the advice he gave is equally appropriate for church leaders introducing this ministry today: *I am sending you out like sheep among wolves. Therefore be as shrewd as snakes and as innocent as doves.* (Matt 10:16)

Here are some helpful tips for church leaders wanting to introduce this ministry in their church. They have been gleaned from others who have already done so:

Commit yourself to ministering healing in this way on any and every occasion you can, both as you visit people in their homes, and at the very end of services, (once you have said good-bye to most people.) Your example of involvement, and the stories you will have to tell, are indispensable. In giving this ministry credibility and respectability in the church.

Start to teach about this ministry from the Scriptures over a few weeks consecutively. Have people give testimony to healings they have received in answer to prayer. These don't have to be spectacular – they simply need to be from people that members of the church can relate to in such a way that they think 'if that happened to them it could happen to me'.

If possible agree with your leadership team that this ministry is so important that it should be done in an orderly and effective way. In this way gain their permission and blessing. If they give it they will help to build an environment of faith. If they resist this ministry, in the long term they may create an environment of doubt and scepticism which can hinder the working of 'mighty miracles', as it did for Jesus in his home town.

Train a ministry team. This training should be advertised publicly so that anyone can come. It is important for the leader to recruit personally and privately to it anyone they really want to be involved. If you are not confident in preparing other material this booklet could be used as an outline for a training course. Alternatively you can form a group to listen to teaching tapes together (available from New Wine). The teaching can be discussed together and then the group can pray for each other. New Wine is also happy to commend other church leaders who have been involved in this ministry for a while and who can come and take a Healing Training Day in your locality. We normally encourage a hosting church to invite other interested people and churches in their locality to join them for this training. If you would like to do this please contact New Wine Networks, c/o St Barnabas Church, Holden Road, London N12 7DN. Tel: 020 8343 6130.

Decide when and where you are going to offer this ministry. Many churches now do so at the end of every main service. Also decide where in the building you will do this. Some like to have it in a side-chapel, and some keep it highly visible at the front of the aisle. While the former offers anonymity, the latter keeps it as a publicly visible ministry. There are advantages and disadvantages in both, but try to do it in a place and way that enables people to see that this ministry is quite 'normal', and not 'special'.

Appoint and authorise the team, and a responsible team leader, in a public service. The team leaders should be well respected by the congregation. It can help at such a public launch to have a visiting speaker, whom you know to be committed to this ministry and with the same New Wine values that you have.

Don't test the Lord. Sometimes in the early days of this ministry a highly visible member of the church becomes ill, and they become a sort of 'test case' in the church to see if this ministry really works. Apart from being in direct disobedience to this command, treating them in this way violates the value of love for the individual.

From time to time invite a speaker and a ministry team from another church to your regular team training evening and/or to one of your church services, or a special Celebration. Knowing there will be a special emphasis on prayer for healing gives church members the extra courage to bring their sick friends, and releases an extra degree of expectation and faith.

Keep recruiting new people into the team, by personal invitation, and by offering training days or courses. If you offer healing prayer ministry at, or after, all your main services you will find that over a period of time God will start bringing people to your church who want to be healed, and you will need a larger pool of people willing to spend time ministering healing to others.

If possible, from time to time get the whole church to minister to each other during a Sunday Service. This ministry is for every Christian and not just for those 'on the ministry team'. Over time it is remarkably easy for the ministry team to become the only people involved in this ministry, and become a sort of closed shop. If this is allowed to happen the potential of this ministry is never realised.

Work with your small group leaders to ensure that they understand the vision and values that you have for this ministry, and that they are allowing space and time for it in their small groups. A well-run small group can offer a 'safe learning environment' where people can first learn to move in the gifts of the Spirit, and start to minister healing. However it is unwise to insist that every group must offer this ministry. It may be too threatening for some church members and we don't want to drive them away.

Persevere – there may not be any spectacular healings for a while. When John Wimber pioneered this ministry in his church it was nine months before anyone experienced any measure of healing as a direct answer to their prayers. Fortunately many churches have not had to wait this long before seeing the Lord bring healing through this ministry!

Selecting the Ministry Team

While we want to encourage every Christian to be involved in the healing ministry, we need to ensure that the ministry we offer to people at public services in church has some sort of credibility. Therefore the church leader should set up some sort of training course, and have a means to vet and authorise those involved.

For various reasons this ministry can sometimes attract people who may not yet be ready to be involved. In training and appointing people we recommend looking for those who are:

Committed to following Jesus – evidenced both by a degree of understanding in their Christian faith, and the fruit of the Spirit being seen in their lifestyle

Wanting to be continuously filled with the Holy Spirit, and prayerfully seeking and using the gifts of the Spirit in ministry.

On their own journey to wholeness, and asking for healing ministry for themselves from time to time.

Sensitive to people – reacting in acceptance and love, rather than shock and judgment to the sins and traumas in which people so easily get trapped.

Committed to the church fellowship, and preferably part of one of the small groups – this indicates a real willingness to live in relationship with others.

Willing to work under the authority of the church and ministry team leaders, and to adhere to the values, guidelines, and practises that the church has adopted for public ministry.

Relatively 'respected' by and 'acceptable' to others in the church.

Sometimes those who are new to the faith and the church are the most teachable about this ministry; they have no 'previous religious experience' which could have given them an alternative theology, value system, and practice. So don't simply look to those who have been in the church for many years. At the same time if there are some on the team who are 'stalwarts' of the church, then this ministry can quickly gain credibility with others who have been around in the church for a long time but for whom the idea of Healing Prayer Ministry is initially quite strange, or even too threatening.

4.2 In a Special Time of Outpouring of the Spirit

Over the last few years there have been some occasions when churches have experienced major visitations of the Holy Spirit, resulting in many people coming for prayer for general renewal and a refreshing of their walk with God. These times have often been accompanied by powerful manifestations, such as shaking, falling, laughing, weeping, and loud cries.

During these times individuals go through powerful experiences of meeting God. These often result in repentance over sin, in greater awareness of God's love, in deepening adoration of Jesus, and in healing of life's hurts. There is often a great sense of awe at being in the presence of a Holy God.

In such times prayer ministry should be exercised upon the same values as outlined earlier, but with even greater sensitivity to what the Holy Spirit is doing. A very helpful opening prayer is: 'Father I bless what you are doing in this person's life.'

It is also helpful to be able to pray biblical prayers, such as these – as the Spirit leads:

To be filled with the Spirit: *(Eph 5:18) Be filled with the Spirit.*

To know God better: *(Eph 1:17) I ..ask..that God .. may give you the Spirit of wisdom and revelation, so that you may know him better.*

To let the light overcome the darkness: *(Eph 1:18) I pray also that the eyes of your heart may be enlightened.*

To know even more of God's love: *(Eph 3:18) And I pray that you,...may...grasp how wide and long and high and deep is the love of Christ.*

To have renewed joy: *(Ps 51:12) Restore...the joy of your salvation.*

To have inner strength: *(Eph 3:16) I pray that out of his glorious riches God may strengthen you with power through his Spirit in your inner being.*

To know God's peace always:*(2 Thess 3:16) Now may the Lord of peace himself give you peace at all times and in every way.*

To live a holy life: *(Col 1:10) And we pray...that you may live a life worthy of the Lord and may please him in every way.*

To bring glory to Jesus: *(2 Thess 1:12) We pray...that the name of our Lord Jesus may be glorified in you.*

To know God's will and calling: *(Matt 6:10) Your kingdom come, your will be done on earth as it is in heaven.*

To be anointed in their calling: *(Acts 13:2) The Holy Spirit said, "Set apart for me Barnabas and Saul for the work to which I have called them." So after they had fasted and prayed, they placed their hands on them and sent them off.*

To share their faith: *(Philemon :6) I pray that you may be active in sharing your faith.*

To know God's protection: *(John 17:15) My prayer is not that you take them out of the world but that you protect them from the evil one.*

For Grace to persevere: *(2 Cor 13:14) May the grace of the Lord Jesus Christ, and the love of God, and the fellowship of the Holy Spirit be with you.*

As in every other setting the ministry is always helped by asking a question at some stage about what the Lord is doing or saying, and asking whether there is anything specific the person is seeking God for, and for which you can pray. But in times of great outpouring of the Spirit many people are quite happy to 'soak' in the presence of God without specific prayer, and those ministering need to allow this to happen without constant interruption.

4.3 In a Conference Setting

All this prayer ministry is about co-operating with God. In a conference setting it is important also to co-operate with the person coordinating the ministry from the front. Learning to listen to their instructions, as well as looking around and 'seeing what God is doing', while at the same time being sensitive to the prompting of the Spirit as you minister to an individual, is an art!

As in other settings it is always good to minister in pairs, ensuring that there is at least one person of the same sex as the person you are ministering to. Take particular care in a crowd not to invade someone's 'space'.

Be careful not to confuse a display of emotion with an evil spirit. It is better to begin ministry on the assumption that repressed hurt is being manifested. It is best not to tell a person they have an evil spirit, even if you think they have! Deliverance can often be done without any obvious 'naming' and 'shouting' at demons. They are simply driven out by the power of God.

Be sensitive to those who are quietly seeking God, rather than ministering only to those who are obviously manifesting 'noisily'. A large crowd can 'encourage' some emotional types to attract attention to themselves, in a way that diverts the ministry team from looking out for those who are hungrily seeking God in other ways. These less obvious people are equally important. (See Matt 9:20-22 – the woman touching Jesus' robes.)

Introduce yourself by name, and discover their name if you don't know it already. Ask if you can pray for them. Being natural and friendly helps puts people at ease with you.

Encourage anyone on whom you 'see the Spirit resting' to open themselves further to his work in them. Assure them that God is good, and that all his plans and purposes for them are good. Some may be afraid of intimacy with God, or of opening up to him emotionally in front of others. Create a safe place around them, and encourage them appropriately, 'Don't be afraid'; 'It's OK to express your feelings'; 'You can stop at any time, but try to go with it'.

Remember people need to take responsibility for their own life and response to God. Wherever possible get them to pray out aloud for what they are seeking, This ensures they are not just expecting us to 'wave a magic wand' over them so that everything will get better. As the ministry progresses their own involvement in discerning what God is doing is important; they have even more responsibility to hear from the Lord than do those ministering.

Don't let people become dependent on you by promising that you will pray for them personally at the next meeting of the conference. Assure them that this is God's work, and that he can continue through the times of worship, and teaching, as well as through the prayers of anyone else on the ministry team. This helps people to look to God as their healer rather than to the advise/help of another human being. Sometimes God begins a work at a conference that he intends to continue in the local church where a continuing relationship with a particular person on the Pastoral Prayer Ministry team may be important. This may be appropriate in the local church but we don't encourage it at conferences.

If you find yourself 'out of your depth' in a particular prayer encounter don't hesitate to ask for help from someone else with more experience.

4.4 In the Community

In the days of the early Jerusalem church the whole community brought their sick for healing, and some exceptional things were happening: *As a result, people brought the sick into the streets and laid them on beds and mats so that at least Peter's shadow might fall on some of them as he passed by. Crowds gathered also from the towns around Jerusalem, bringing their sick and those tormented by evil spirits, and all of them were healed. (Acts 5:15-16)*

Healings were not confined to those who were already Christians. Some were healed and then subsequently gave their lives to Jesus Christ as Saviour and Lord. Similarly in our generation this ministry should not be confined to within the walls of our church buildings and the community of the converted. 'The meeting place is the learning place for the market place.' We believe the church needs to have both a model for healing which is easy to use outside the church building, and also a renewed confidence to offer to minister healing anywhere and everywhere we go. Our homes, our places of work, the school gate, our social clubs, trains, planes, and even the supermarket, are all places where in natural conversation we can offer to minister healing to anyone who is sick. John Wimber used to insist 'The meat is in the street.'

The Lord added to their number daily those who were being saved. (Acts 2:47). One of the reasons for the growth of the early church was the remarkable healing ministry that was happening. Around the world today where churches are rediscovering the healing ministry – and it is in its rightful place alongside the teaching, evangelistic, prophetic and pastoral ministry of the church – then they too are growing steadily. God adds to their number those being saved.

If healings were taking place both in our local churches up and down the country, and in the communities served by our churches, then there would surely be a stirring in the nation. These healings will happen if church leaders and members alike commit themselves to seeking the presence and power of the Lord of glory, and if they are willing to rediscover and pursue the ministry of Jesus as outlined earlier in this booklet.

A church leader recently made a comment to this effect: 'Signs and wonders occur on the frontier between the Kingdom of God and the dominion of darkness. If you are not seeing signs and wonders ask yourself if you are any longer on the frontier.'

We pray that as you commit yourself and your church to living 'on the frontier' you will have the joy of seeing God at work in healing those to whom you minister, and also the privilege of being part of a church which is growing in number to the glory of God.

About The Author

John Coles is the leader of New Wine – a movement committed to 'Equipping churches to see Jesus Kingdom Grow'. He is the non-stipendiary incumbent of St Barnabas, Finchley where he was the Vicar for 20 years. During that time he saw God change and grow the church from its small, sleepy, and liberal beginnings to a large multinational biblically based church, which has become a resourcing church in North London and within the New Wine Network of churches. John's ministry is now mainly to other church leaders in envisioning, encouraging and empowering them to lead their churches through similar changes to those at St Barnabas.

St. Barnabas is distinctly informal in style, with a strong emphasis on worship, teaching from the Bible, and the power of God to change people's lives. Broken and wounded people have come from a wide area of north London and many have been significantly healed. John wants to see other churches experience renewal under the Holy Spirit as they have at St. Barnabas. He is aware he has made many mistakes along the way, and wants to help others to avoid them! He is also committed to starting new churches, with different styles, to reach other cultures.

John is married to Anne who was for many years the worship director at St Barnabas. She is now the Ministry Pastor at the church, in addition to being involved in the ministry of New Wine, especially in the development of women in leadership. They have 4 children aged 16-23.

Since attending some of John Wimber's conferences in the mid-eighties, and with encouragement from David Pytches, John has been learning how to minister healing in his church of St Barnabas, Woodside Park. He has implemented the principles he talked about, and seen many people experience significant emotional, spiritual and physical healing through the healing ministry that he has encouraged and led during his 20 years as Vicar.

For more information about New Wine Networks contact:
New Wine Networks, c/o St Barnabas Church, Holden Road, London N12, England. Tel: 020 8343 6130.

New Wine Vision

We want to see as many Christians and churches as possible alive with the joy of knowing and worshipping Jesus Christ, and equipped to live out and proclaim his kingdom in the love of God the Father and the power and gifts of the Holy Spirit.

New Wine Mission

Through the Holy Spirit, we seek fulfilment of this vision by means of:

Summer family conferences that aim to envision and empower Christians and churches for worship which is passionate, intimate, reverent and biblical; for ministry in the power and gifts of the Spirit, modelled in a mature, responsible way; for teaching through Bible expositions and a breadth of seminar options, as a means to equip them for Spirit-filled Christian life and ministry in their churches and where they live and work.

The work of the New Wine Network that provides local relational support, training and encouragement for like-minded leaders across the UK and other nations. In addition to the annual National Leaders' Conference, training conferences (1-3 days in length) are held all around the Network. We also place strategic emphasis on training church leaders through New Wine Leaders' Retreats and other training events.

Encouraging national and international faith-sharing visits to churches that are seeking to grow in renewal, by leaders and other teachers taking out teams of people from their churches.

Seeking to discern where the Spirit is leading in issues of social responsibility, justice, community and the environment. Teaching on these issues is an important part of the seminar programmes at the Shepton Mallet summer gatherings.

Encouraging church planting and other church-based initiatives to reach the unchurched in our increasingly postmodern society.

Helping the poor both in this country and beyond through the local church and our conferences.

Publishing New Wine Magazine and books, booklets and other teaching materials such as videos and tapes as a further means of propagating teaching that adheres to New Wine values.

Serving traditional churches, both in this country and abroad, that are seeking to grow in renewal. Although New Wine started amongst those seeking renewal within the Church of England, we now have the privilege of serving many other denominations.

New Wine, 4a Ridley Avenue, Ealing, London W13 9XW, England
Tel: 020 8567 6717 www.new-wine.org